# PRAYING
# IN EXILE

# PRAYING IN EXILE

GORDON MURSELL

DARTON · LONGMAN + TODD

BV
4911
.M87
2005

First published in 2005 by
Darton, Longman and Todd Ltd
1 Spencer Court
140–142 Wandsworth High Street
London
SW18 4JJ

ISBN 0–232–52228–6

A catalogue record for this book is available from the British Library.

The Scripture quotations in this publication are taken from
the New Revised Standard Version © 1989, 1995. Division of
Christian Education of the National Council of the Churches of
Christ in the United States of America.
Extracts from the Psalms are taken from *Common Worship:
Daily Prayer* (London: Church House Publishing, 2002).


Phototypeset by Intype Libra Ltd
Printed and bound in Great Britain by
Page Bros, Norwich, Norfolk

In loving memory of my parents
Philip Riley Mursell (1918–65)
Sheena Nicolson Mursell (1917–2001).

# CONTENTS

# ACKNOWLEDGEMENTS

It has been an immense privilege for me to have been actively involved in the planning of Celebrating Sanctuary Birmingham, the annual Refugee Week celebrations, during the past three years. I owe a great debt both to the other organizers and to the many refugees and asylum seekers whom I have come to know as a result.

This book would have been impossible without the love and support (not to mention the forbearance) of my wife, Anne.

The extract from the poem 'The Hijrah to God' by Nazik al-Mala'ika, translated by Basima Bezirgan, Elizabeth Fernea, Ferial J. Ghazoul, Ibtisam S. Barakat, Saleh Alyafai and Jenna Abdul, appears by kind permission of the editors of *Iraqi Poetry Today*, published by King's College London.

The extract from the song 'This Nearly was Mine' (words by Oscar Hammerstein II, music by Richard Rodgers), © 1949 Williamson Music International USA, appears by kind permission of EMI Music Publishing Ltd, London WC2H 0QY.

Permission has been sought for the use of the extract from the song 'California Dreamin'', © 1966 Universal Music (UK), Ltd, London W6 9XS.

The extract from *I have not seen a butterfly around here: children's drawings and poems from Terezín* is © The Jewish

Museum Prague 1993 and reproduced by kind permission of the Museum.

The extract from the speech by Allan Pettersson, from the translation given in the sleeve note for CD number 992 224-2, produced by CPO, Lübecker Strasse 9, D-49124 Georgsmarienhütte, Germany, is reproduced by kind permission of CPO.

# CHAPTER ONE

## *What Is Exile?*

I was born in Guildford, and brought up in the prosperous commuter countryside of Surrey and West Sussex. My memories of childhood are, for the most part, happy ones, and I have little doubt that my parents gave me and my younger brother an upbringing that was both secure and genuinely loving. I could never be too grateful for that, although I took it for granted at the time, and this book is dedicated to their memory.

But when I was eight years old, my parents sent me to a boarding school, 100 miles away on the Kent coast. I can recall little about the first term: the sheer grim strangeness of the experience was enough to keep me occupied. But I remember with unsparing clarity the beginning of the second: at Victoria Station in London, where parents entrusted their offspring, neatly turned out in their grey uniforms with shorts and caps to the school staff, I rebelled, and fought like a tiny cornered cat to prevent the handover from taking place. 'I don't want to go!' I protested. 'Why do I have to go?' My father became embarrassed, and my mother upset. This wasn't what was supposed to happen. In the end the school staff bundled me aboard, and I went. But, for me at least, my question was left hanging unanswered in the air, and in some respects it hangs there still.

I was experiencing exile, though it would be many years before I would call it that, and by then I would come to see that it was a very privileged form of exile by comparison with that of millions of others. But that didn't make it feel any less real at the time. I will argue in this book that exile is any situation or

1

experience in which you are not at home, and not in control of what is happening to you. It is one of the most common of all aspects of creaturely life (I use the word 'creaturely' advisedly, since it extends well beyond the human), and it has its roots in two of the most fundamental of all experiences, birth and migration.

The recognition that exile begins at birth is set out with infinite subtlety at the very beginning of the Bible. God creates by speaking the divine Word into the primal watery chaos described in the mysterious and majestic opening verses of Genesis. The Word brings forth identity, order, pattern and meaning as it encounters and addresses the chaos. And it does this in three stages: by *celebrating*, *separating*, and *naming* what is being created.

The *celebrating* comes first: 'And God saw that [it] was good' (Gen. 1:4). In the words of John D. Davies, God's work of creation 'begins in a head-on confrontation between God and every kind of disorder. God comes into the story as critic, and his first word is a word of doom to the *status quo*.'[1] Each act of creation is an act of defiance, wresting new life and hope from a chaos which represents pure potential for both good and evil: if it is not addressed and worked on by the divine Word, the chaos, which always exists both within and outside us, has the capacity to overwhelm us – as indeed it does five chapters later in the story of Noah. This is one of the reasons why the Hebrew poets drew so frequently on the image of drowning to describe any experience of dereliction or despair. It is also why we can never spend too long celebrating what the Mexican poet Octavio Paz calls 'the dark forgotten marvel of being alive'.[2]

The *naming* is the third stage of creation. 'And God called the light Day, and the darkness he called Night' (Gen. 1:5). Names make possible not only identity, but relationship; the child learns about both by giving names to everything he or she encounters. The ability to name a hitherto indescribable fear or fantasy allows us to grapple with it instead of being possessed by it, which is why the writer of Psalm 39 refuses to keep silence in the midst of great evil:

I held my tongue and said nothing:
I kept silent but found no comfort.

2

My pain was increased – my heart grew hot within me:
while I mused the fire blazed and I spoke with my tongue . . .
  (Ps. 39:3)

Furthermore, the names God gives to creatures in Scripture are oriented to the future, not to the past: so Abram and Sarai become Abraham and Sarah when a new vocation is opened up to them, and the elderly woman Elizabeth defies convention by giving her infant son a name that has nothing to do with his ancestors, but everything to do with his future: 'he is to be called John [the Baptist]' (Luke 1:60). So too, Jesus gives new names to those whom he is inviting to join him in a new future which is unimaginably different from where they have come from: ' "You are Simon son of John. You are to be called Cephas" (which is translated Peter)' (John 1:42).

Between the celebrating and the naming comes the crucial middle stage of God's work of creation: *separating*. 'And God separated the light from the darkness' (Gen. 1:4), and God goes on to separate the waters below the firmament from those above it, the male from the female, the weekday from the sabbath, and so on. This process of separation has nothing to do with autonomy: a closer analogy is the act of giving birth, when the child is separated from his or her mother's womb precisely so that he or she may be capable of identity and relationship. Yet separation is costly, because it demands of the new-born creature the willingness to leave home and to enter a strange new world of unfamiliar sights and sounds.

So birth is our first experience of exile, of not being at home and not being in control of what is happening, and our first response is instructive. We *protest*, and (albeit reluctantly at first) we *adapt* to our new surroundings. We shall explore both of these in more detail later. We shall also explore an even more instructive feature of that first encounter with exile, a stern but crucial truth about creaturely life which the Bible has much to say about: the discovery that we can never go *back* home. The past is as irrecoverable as the womb from which we came. For the moment, though, we need to touch on the second primary root of all our experiences of exile: migration.

The urge to migrate, either in search of food or shelter or to

3

escape from adversity, is also central to creaturely life. In Genesis, God commands the birds to 'fly above the earth across the dome of the sky' (1:20), and the experience of migration remains common to innumerable species of bird, fish, mammal and even insect: the ant *Hypoclinea cuspidatus*, for instance, lives a form of nomadic existence in company with the mealybug in the rain forests of Malaysia, and some creatures (like the arctic tern, or the salmon, or the caribou) travel astonishing distances every year. The names we give such creatures are instructive: the peregrine, a kind of falcon, derives its name from the Latin word for being in, or travelling to, a foreign place; the Wandering Albatross, whose immense wingspan allows it to circumnavigate the globe, is recognized as an exile by its Latin description *Diomedea exsulans*; and the Inuit people of Greenland call the polar bear *pihoqahiaq*, 'the ever-wandering one'.

The same urge to migrate has characterized human civilization since earliest times; even today many societies, such as the Inuit or Mongol peoples, reflect (as we shall see in the following chapter) the values of the nomad: the willingness to travel light, to create a sense of home in even the least hospitable places or most transient experiences, to live in ecological symbiosis with livestock and landscape, and to transmit to succeeding generations the stories, customs and accumulated wisdom of their forebears – all these mark out the distinctive spirituality of the migrant or nomad. The Bible knows this too: throughout Scripture there is an enduring tension between the settler and the exile, from the expulsion of Adam and Eve from humanity's first home to the closing vision (itself nurtured by an exile, John of Patmos) of the eternal city whose gates are always open. The people of Israel became economic migrants, driven by oppression from Egypt in search of a new and better life elsewhere; the infant Jesus became, with his parents, an asylum seeker in the very country from which his distant forebears had fled. And (a far more terrible irony) the Bible reminds us that it was precisely those who had themselves known the experience of forced migration who became, on arrival in Canaan, settlers who were ruthlessly capable of driving out those who had been there before them. The same tragic irony exists today, in a world where the descendants of Angles, Jutes, Saxons and other wandering tribes have no hesitation in closing their

4

doors against the economic migrants and asylum seekers of the third millennium.

So the experience of exile is both a central feature of all creaturely existence and a distinctive attribute of many who are poor and oppressed. But it is also shared by millions of creatures (human beings among them) who have felt the urge to seek a better life far from what hitherto they had called home. Those who freely choose to live in a foreign country in response to a lucrative job offer can scarcely be described as exiles in the same way as refugees detained in a European immigration centre can – and yet the former (and to an even greater extent their families) will encounter the distinguishing features of all exile – the fact of not being at home and not being in control – as will the latter. In a fast-moving, fast-changing world, in which the gap between rich and poor constantly increases and the impact of human greed and selfishness on the world's fragile ecosystems increases with it, exile becomes more, not less common. It is worth concluding this chapter with some examples of it.

The most obvious exemplars of exile are the refugees, who have fled from persecution or discrimination, often with no time to prepare or to say goodbye to loved ones, and with no resources other than what they carry within themselves. Many rapidly discover that their treatment in the countries in which they have sought refuge is not much better than what they experienced in their countries of origin. At worst, they may be sent back to where they came from, or bundled unceremoniously from one state to another while successive immigration departments wash their hands of them. Even at best, they are likely to be the victims of stereotyping and abuse. Here is the experience of Zrinka:

> As a refugee, each time I read the newspapers, it is about me. When I go to the hairdresser even, it's a great conversation killer – when they ask you where you're from and you say Bosnia. There is no escape – 24 hours a day . . . I don't mind that people see me as a refugee – that's what happened to me. But they don't see anything else. They contextualize me in this victim identity. They don't say you are a journalist, you are a director, you are a refugee advocate, they say you are a refugee, which has a negative connotation in the public mind.[3]

5

And this is the experience of Feride, a woman graduate who became a refugee in the United Kingdom:

I wish the skills and knowledge we have were recognised along with our life experiences. I wish we were given a chance to unpack our bags to start using what we have carried with us. I wish we were not made to feel that whatever we learned before was useless and that we should start from scratch. I wish our experiences were valued. We should be given opportunities to contribute more than just cheap labour to the society we now live in.[4]

Both Zrinka and Feride reflect aspirations common to many exiles: the longing to be treated as a human being rather than as a problem or a statistic, and the longing to contribute in some way to the society to which they have come. We shall return to these aspirations later. But it is important to recognize that they are felt by many others who experience exile even without becoming refugees or asylum seekers. Consider, for example, the experience of those bullied at school, who are too terrified to tell their parents for fear of reprisals. That is an experience of exile. So is being a patient in hospital, precipitated into a world of tubes and trolleys and white coats, where the individual is stripped of almost all his or her customary defences and control and exposed to an alarmingly uncertain future. Or being one of a retired couple who, having settled in a new location anticipating a well-deserved lifestyle free from the stresses of paid work, suffers the sudden loss of a beloved spouse and finds him- or herself desperately alone and deprived even of old friends with whom to share memories. Or the experience of ex-prisoners, sustained during the years of incarceration by the prospect of a new life outside, only to find the 'home' to which they return is an entirely different place and they themselves entirely different people. Or the widow beginning to experience the onset of Alzheimer's disease; the migrant worker obliged to leave home to support his or her family; the teenager who ends up homeless in a strange city. For many in past generations, marriage could be a form of exile, usually for the wife: D.H. Lawrence's Mrs Morel, in *Sons and Lovers*, could speak for many when she reflected that 'looking ahead, the prospect of her life made her feel as if she were buried alive . . . "I wait," Mrs Morel said to herself – "I wait, and what I wait for can never come."[5]

And then there are the times when we are rejected or betrayed by someone we loved and trusted, the moments when our emotional landscapes are suddenly turned upside-down as completely as though the pavement had disappeared from under our feet, leaving us with feelings of hurt, anger, and puzzlement (where did I go wrong? what did I say or do?) and of powerless frustration (it could have been so good), not to mention the inevitable damage done to our self-confidence and to our ability ever again to trust someone, or to take the risk of loving someone in the face of another possible rejection.

We must be careful here. It would be quite wrong to suggest that all these experiences (still less that of the middle-class child at boarding school) are comparable in extent or intensity to those of the geographical exile, driven from home and family and all that made life worthwhile into a new and terrifyingly lonely future. And if we render the term 'exile' too inclusive, we risk diluting whatever distinctive meaning it had in the first place. But there is a greater danger: that of so distancing ourselves from the plight and experience of those enduring physical exile that we fail to realize how much we have in common with them, fail to recognize the universality of what it is like to be far from home and without control over what is happening, fail to acknowledge our urgent need to discover what can help us cope with exile when it happens to us. Because it will, and in some sense or other will have done so already. This book is written out of the discovery that exile is something all of us have to face, and out of the conviction that there exist, for those willing to seek them out, priceless spiritual resources to help us do so with hope and not despair.

# CHAPTER TWO

# *Moon River*
## *Being a Nomad*

### *Introduction*

In the film *Breakfast at Tiffany's*, released in 1961, Audrey Hepburn sat on a window-sill and sang (not, it has to be said, very well) a song by Johnny Mercer and Henry Mancini which captured the essence not only of that film but of an entire post-war generation. 'Moon River' would be taken up by greater singers like Frank Sinatra and Danny Williams, but Hepburn had already made it famous. The evocation of the great river, 'wider than a mile', with exciting destinations 'waiting round the bend' for those prepared to go and look for them, caught the mood of all who felt that there must be more to life than war and violence and increasing material prosperity. And the 'two drifters, off to see the world', acutely aware that 'there's such a lot of world to see', can represent far more than the hippies of the 1960s or even the globetrotters of today: they stand for all who have felt restless and confined, their spirit hungry and their potential unfulfilled. 'Moon river and me' – together (it seems to say) we will see the world – and even, maybe, change it.

The dreams and longings evoked by Mercer and Mancini were not new: in fact they must be among the most ancient ever experienced by humanity. They form as good a point of entry as any into the world of the nomad: the word comes from the Greek for 'pasture' and was originally used to describe those who followed their herds in search of food, water and safety, though it came to denote anyone who lived a wandering life. The nomad and the

8

exile are not the same thing: the Jews were not nomads in Babylon – any more than others forced to settle where they are not at home – though they were certainly exiles. Yet the two have much in common: nomads may appear, to the romantic or the prisoner or the commuter, to be free spirits, 'off to see the world'. But they do not usually do so for fun: they do so because they have no choice – and 'lack of choice', as a Palestinian woman wrote, 'is what exile is all about'.[1] The children of Israel could have stayed on as slaves in Egypt and rejected the call of Moses and Aaron to seek the promised land: later, many of them wished they had. But it was not much of a choice: and in becoming nomads, or what is today disdainfully described as 'economic migrants', they were doing no more and no less than what all human beings – indeed all creatures – seek to do: the best they can for themselves and their kin. Like the exile, the nomad has to live with transience, with being in places where you are not at home and not in control, and with the discovery that many doors are closed against you. In what follows we shall explore something of what it means to be a nomad, of what it may mean to see ourselves as nomads, and of what the Bible can teach us about how to make sense of both.

### *The Nomad in the Bible*

The tension between the settler and the nomad runs, as we have seen, throughout the Bible. Abram is called by God from his settled life at Haran: he is told to 'go from' his country and his father's house, but not told where he is to 'go to' (Gen.12:1) – only that he is to be made into a great nation. This is the originating character of the biblical nomad, called into a new and uncertain yet exciting future, but one that is not under his or her control. Sometimes it is not so much exciting as terrifying, as when the slave-woman Hagar is twice driven out by the jealous Sarah (Gen.16 and 21), facing death in the desert with her infant son until God hears the cry of the child and saves them both. Like the exile, however, they do not go back home, but instead survive and grow in the wilderness (Gen. 21:20–2).

Two other stories allow us to explore further the spirituality of the nomad. Moses becomes a nomad almost at birth, when his mother sets him adrift on the Nile in Egypt in the hope of avoiding Pharaoh's ruthless order to exterminate all male Israelite children (Exod. 2). Later he flees into exile from Egypt after killing an Egyptian who was beating one of his kinsfolk; when his first child is born, he names him Gershom (from the Hebrew word *ger*, meaning a sojourner or nomad), for, as Moses says, 'I have been an alien [*ger*] residing in a foreign land' (Exod. 2:22). Yet it is this wandering fugitive who is called by God to set God's people free, and Moses will spend the rest of his life as a nomad, dying in sight of (but outside) the promised land to which he had led his fellow Israelites (Deut. 34). Like millions today, Moses' life is threatened from the moment of his birth: he is an alien in a dangerous world, powerless and alone. Yet it is this man, a stateless outcast and an ex-murderer, a serious threat to the status quo, whom God summons through the medium of the burning bush to be the instrument of the divine purpose. And, in the long journey to freedom, Moses becomes not just God's servant but God's friend, wrestling with God in the clouds on the summit of Sinai as he had once wrestled in the sand with a brutal Egyptian (Exod. 32:11–14).

The second story is that of Ruth, a young Moabite woman who marries an economic migrant from the land of Judah: when her husband dies, Ruth is left with her mother-in-law Naomi, whom she refuses to abandon. Instead, in a remarkable act of altruism, Ruth makes herself into an alien, a *ger*, by travelling with Naomi back to Naomi's home town of Bethlehem, in order to create a new future for both of them.[2] When they arrive there, Naomi tells the townsfolk not to call her 'Naomi' (meaning 'pleasant') any longer, but instead to call her 'Mara' (meaning 'bitter'), for, as she says, 'the Almighty has dealt bitterly with me. I went away full, but the Lord has brought me back empty' (Ruth 1:20–1). Yet no one calls her by that terrible new name: instead they hold fast to the name and the identity she already possessed. In the moving story that follows, we are shown how this return home is not a going back in despair but a going forward in hope, as the two bereaved and powerless women bring about a new future not only for themselves but for the world, since Ruth's child Obed is the ancestor of both David and Jesus (Ruth 4:17, 21).[3]

Moses and Ruth: these two unlikely people, left exposed and adrift by circumstances beyond their control, remain nomads,

10

outsiders: yet they also become crucial agents of change, instrumental in opening up a new future for those around them. This is often the legacy of the nomad. In his exploration of the historical achievement of the Mongols (who with the Bedouin tribes of the Middle East remain to this day arguably the most genuinely nomadic people in the contemporary world), Stanley Stewart underlines two enduring characteristics of the nomad. The first is hospitality: 'nomad tents have big doors' is the remark of one nomadic chief whom Stewart quotes,[4] and he goes on to record the horror of contemporary Mongolians on hearing that one has to pay for a cup of tea in the United Kingdom.[5] The second is the ability to make connections, to bring people and ideas together. Writing of the legacy of the terrible Genghis Khan, the greatest and most famous Mongol of all time, Stewart points out that the vast empire left behind by this astonishing nomadic ruler collapsed within a hundred years, bequeathing scarcely any buildings or other visible signs of its existence. Yet it achieved something no less enduring: it put east and west in touch with one another, creating contacts and opening up possibilities which later generations could and would develop:

> By pushing beyond their own ill-defined frontiers, the nomads of the steppe had set the whole world in motion. It was their historic role, to provoke change among the settled peoples whose societies they disrupted. When eventually the Mongols returned home, they went back to their old life, as if nothing had happened. For the rest of the world, nothing would be the same again.[6]

### *The* Ger

It is striking to note that the Hebrew word for 'sojourner', 'nomad' or 'stranger' (*ger*) is the same as the Mongol word for the nomad's tent. In the Hebrew Bible (or Old Testament), it is made clear again and again that the people of God are to honour the sojourner, first because that is what God does and, second, because they were all once sojourners themselves: '[God] executes justice for the orphan and the widow, and . . . loves the strangers [*ger*], providing them

11

with food and clothing. You shall also love the stranger, for you were strangers in the land of Egypt' (Deut. 10:18–19). Reverencing the nomad in this way will bring blessings on them all (notice here the identification of the *ger* with the Levitical priest, who could own no land, and with other marginal people):

> At the end of every third year you are to bring out all the tithe of your produce for that year and leave it in your settlements so that the Levites, who have no holding of ancestral land among you, and the aliens [*ger*], orphans, and widows in your settlements may come and have plenty to eat. If you do this the Lord your God will bless you in everything to which you set your hand. (Deut. 14:28–9 REB)

In the Psalms, the spiritual significance of the *ger* becomes clear. First, this is someone whom God cares about: 'The Lord loves the righteous: the Lord cares for the stranger [*ger*] in the land' (Ps. 146:9). Hence the outrage of the psalmist when others fail to show the same care: 'They murder the widow and the alien [*ger*]: they put the fatherless to death' (Ps. 94:6). For the truth is, as we have already seen, that all of us are strangers on earth: 'For I am but a stranger [*ger*] with you: a passing guest as all my forebears were' (Ps. 39:12).

For Christians, it is only through the sheer graciousness of God in Christ, redeeming us and making us God's children, that we can see ourselves and one another as strangers no longer: 'So then you are no longer strangers and aliens, but you are citizens with the saints and also members of the household of God' (Eph. 2:19).[7]

Yet in an irreducible sense we do remain strangers: the writer of the Letter to the Hebrews refers to all our forebears in the faith as 'strangers and foreigners on the earth', people who are seeking a homeland, a city, that is always ahead in the future (Heb. 11:13–16). We shall return to this theme in our final chapter. And the First Letter of Peter is explicitly addressed to 'God's scattered people' (in Greek 'the chosen exiles of the diaspora'), dwelling temporarily in a wide range of places, whom the writer will later describe as 'aliens and exiles', temporary residents in the world around them. This fundamental sense of transience, of never fully being at home where we are, is part of our spiritual make-up, part of the restlessness that is at the heart of our vocation as human beings.

## *Psalm 119*

Perhaps the most interesting reference to the *ger* appears in one of the greatest and least-understood spiritual texts in the Judaeo-Christian tradition: Psalm 119. This immensely long prayer is often dismissed, either because of its plethora of synonyms for 'law' – testimonies, statutes, commandments, and so on – one or other of which appears in virtually every verse, or because of the psalm's almost hypnotic repetitiveness. Both these criticisms miss the point, and it is important for our purposes to see why. The synonyms for law come alive when we realize that 'law' is a poor translation for the rich Hebrew word *torah*, which means something more like God's providential teaching, direction or instruction for the people of God. The fact that this most personal and seemingly introspective of psalms focuses constantly on God's *torah* underlines something often lost to sight in twenty-first-century Christian spirituality: a refusal to separate prayer from justice, spiritual life from ethical and moral behaviour, the individual from the corporate. This great prayer is the mirror-opposite of a narrow or comfortable self-absorption. You cannot come closer to God without also coming closer to your neighbour.

And the reason for this brings us to the second criticism often made of Psalm 119. The careful alphabetical structure (the psalm is divided into twenty-two sections, each comprising eight verses, with the verses of each section all beginning with the same letter of the Hebrew alphabet) and deliberately repetitive character point strongly to the origins of this psalm in Israel's experience of exile: for both structure and character serve to make the individual verses and sections easier to memorize. As Rabbi Hugo Gryn, himself a survivor of Auschwitz, pointed out, the people of Israel could not take their religious sanctuaries with them into exile, so they had to create, so to speak, portable sanctuaries, spiritual rucksacks – stories, hopes, memories and texts that had been learnt by heart and could be called to mind at will. We shall explore these spiritual resources in more detail in the chapters that follow. What matters now is that it is the experience of exile which almost certainly gives Psalm 119 its distinctive structure and tone.[8] It consists of 176 verses, each a prayer that is complete in itself, each containing three clear foci – the self, the *torah*, and the Lord – each designed to be learned by heart and called to mind when needed. In a frenetic, unreflective age like ours, we have largely lost this ruminative capacity to learn spiritual texts by heart, and are infinitely the poorer for it – especially when we are ourselves in exile.

In one verse of Psalm 119 the word *ger* appears explicitly:

I am but a stranger [*ger*] on the earth:
do not hide your commandments from me. (v. 19)

Yet the experience of the nomad colours nearly every verse. The entire psalm reflects the sense of being on a journey, from the opening verse to the closing one. The opening verse is:

Blessed are those whose way is blameless:
who walk in the law of the Lord. (v. 1)

The Hebrew word translated 'blessed' comes from a root meaning 'one who makes progress'. So to be 'blessed' is not to enjoy some kind of static perfection, but to have a goal in life, to know where you are going and why – as opposed to sinners, who have lost their way and wandered off. This opening verse sets the tone for what follows: this is not academic reflection for the scribe, but food for the journey of the nomad and the exile, who need all the help and wisdom they can get if they are to walk in the right direction. References to walking, to 'the way' and to the risk of getting lost recur throughout the psalm, not least in its closing verse:

I have gone astray like a sheep that is lost:
O seek your servant, for I do not forget your commandments.
    (v. 176)

And it is God's 'commandments', the *torah*, that collectively constitute the primary item in the exile's rucksack: the shared stories and accumulated wisdom of the people of God, the painful memories and astonishing experiences of grace, the inherited sense of a moral and ethical compass for our journeyings, and above all the enduring conviction that we never travel alone. The

14

*torah* of Psalm 119 allows the nomad to defy the powerful ('I shall speak of your commands before kings: and shall not be put to shame', v. 46), and to sing as he or she walks ('Your statutes have become my songs', v. 54): it sustains the nomad at times of terrible emptiness and despair ('I am parched as a wineskin in the smoke: yet I do not forget your statutes', v. 83); it allows the nomad to embrace a larger, cosmic perspective ('Lord, your word is for ever: it stands firm in the heavens: your faithfulness abides from one generation to another, firm as the earth which you have made', vv. 89–90); it is a source not only of wisdom but of sweetness (v. 103), delight (v. 92), shelter (v. 114), 'a lantern to my feet' (v. 105) and a source of endless *surprise*: 'I am as glad of your word as one who finds rich spoil' (v. 162).[9] Finally, this holding-fast to *torah* on a lonely journey into exile allows the psalmist to glimpse a new future even in the midst of despair:

> My lips shall pour forth your praise:
> because you teach me your statutes. (v. 171)

None of this is to imply that the experience of being a nomad is invariably, or even commonly, easy or comfortable. One of the other striking characteristics of Psalm 119 is the intense language of desire it contains, the passionate longing for meaning and hope and a sense of purpose in the midst of uncertainty, a recurring conviction that *something has gone wrong*, that life should not be like this:

> I have sought you with my whole heart (v. 10)
>
> My soul is consumed with longing (v. 20)
>
> I am humbled to the dust (v. 25)
>
> My soul pines away for sorrow (v. 28)
>
> My soul languishes for your salvation (v. 81)
>
> My eyes fail with watching for your promise:
> saying 'O when will you comfort me?' (v. 82)

All is not what it seems: beneath the seemingly placid, structured formality of Psalm 119 is an encyclopaedia of human experience, a treasury of wisdom for the life of the nomad, a strategy for survival in a dangerous and unpredictable world. The emphasis on order and law and the tightly controlled structure are not accidental: if we recall the fundamental Jewish notion of creation out of chaos, discussed in the previous chapter, we should not need reminding that the people of God embarked on their journeys with a heightened awareness that disorder and chaos were always within and around them, always threatening to engulf and destroy them. The discipline and coherence of Psalm 119 are analogous to the contrapuntal masterpieces of J.S. Bach: in both, structure and spontaneity, intellect and emotion, order and freedom, are held together in a tension that alone nourishes both mind and heart. For both the exile and the nomad, nothing less will do:

> Let me run the way of your commandments:
> for you will liberate my heart. (v. 32)

### *Jesus the Nomad*

The Psalms as a whole have one further contribution to make to the spirituality of the nomad: the recognition that, in a profound sense, God is a nomad too. '[God] will cover you with his wings and you will be safe under his feathers: his faithfulness will be your shield and defence' (Ps. 91:4). At the shrine of Our Lady in the Pyrenean town of Lourdes, where in 1858 the Virgin Mary is believed to have appeared to a local teenager, Bernadette Soubirous, a new chapel of Perpetual Adoration has been built directly opposite the grotto itself. In it, the Blessed Sacrament is reserved, not in a grand tabernacle on the altar but in a light and slender sculpture suspended from the roof, which represents the pillar of fire that was believed to have gone ahead of the people of Israel during the Exodus. Why? As a reminder that God too is a nomad, as really present to us on our journeys as in any religious shrines or churches.[10] The image of God as a bird, explicit here in Psalm 91, is one way of representing this truth. Another can be found in what the Gospels tell us about Jesus.

It requires no idealizing of the nomadic condition to recognize that many of its most enduring and attractive characteristics are found in the Gospel accounts of Jesus. The *hospitalité du coeur*

16

practised by the Mongols and all other nomadic peoples, the ability to make connections and to open up hitherto undreamed-of possibilities, the refusal to separate the individual from the community, spirituality from justice – all these figure prominently in the Gospels, as well as other nomadic characteristics, some of which are explored more fully below: a love of stories and capacity for story-telling, a willingness to live unpossessively and in a symbiotic relationship with one's natural environment, a willingness to travel to where need or sustenance are to be found, and to resist the easy and exclusive certainties of the settler. Jesus was born and died 'outside the city gate' (Heb. 13:12); he spent his entire ministry on the road, and had nowhere to lay his head; and he commissioned his first disciples to go out as nomads, travelling light and living simply as he did. And this brings us to one of the greatest stories in the New Testament, in which the contrast between what we might describe as a nomadic spirituality and a repressively institutional one is powerfully set out: the story in the Gospel of John of the man who was born blind.

### The Story of the Man who Was Born Blind (John 9)

The story opens with words that immediately speak to our theme. 'As [Jesus] walked along, he saw a man blind from birth' (v. 1). Jesus is the nomad, never entirely at home in religious buildings or with the conventionally religious: this story immediately follows the account of how he is forced to leave the Temple by the religious authorities who are outraged at the claims he is making (John 8:48–59). Here he encounters another nomad: a roadside beggar, excluded from society no less than was Jesus but for a different reason. 'Two drifters, off to see the world' – except that one of them cannot see anything, and never had. Like most of the great encounters with Jesus described in the Gospels, this one takes place outside, on the road, where two different kinds of nomad meet one another. The world of organized religion suddenly seems very distant.

Jesus is not the only person to see the blind man. His disciples see him too, but where Jesus sees him as a human being to be addressed and helped, they see him as a theological problem to

17

be talked about and otherwise ignored: 'Rabbi, who sinned, this man or his parents, that he was born blind?' (v. 2). The evangelist is here already beginning to delineate, not just two different ways of seeing, but two different kinds of religion: one (that of the disciples) is primarily interested in *explaining* the world, while the other (that of Jesus) is primarily interested in *changing* it.

Jesus' response to the disciples' question ('Neither this man nor his parents sinned; he was born blind so that God's works might be revealed in him', v. 3) is much controverted: John Hull has acutely argued that 'The man has been born blind in order to provide a sort of photo opportunity for Jesus.'[11] It is certainly possible to read the text in that way, though the words that Jesus goes on to utter suggest a different interpretation: 'We must work the works of him who sent me while it is day; night is coming when no one can work' (v. 4). It is as though Christ is saying: this is not the moment, and there is not the time, to discuss why this man was born blind – other than to insist that his blindness is not caused by his or anyone else's sin. The first and primary response must be to address the man and help him, not to talk about him. No one has more eloquently contrasted the disciples' response to the blind man with that of Jesus than the great Victorian Baptist preacher Charles Spurgeon:

> Cheap moral observations steeped in vinegar make a poor dish for an invalid . . . Whenever you see a man in sorrow and trouble, the way to look at it is, not to blame him and inquire how he came there, but to say, "Here is an opening for God's almighty love. Here is an occasion for the display of the grace and goodness of the Lord." This man being blind gave the Lord Jesus opportunity for the good work of giving him his sight, and that work was so great a wonder that all around were obliged to remark it and admire it. The neighbours began to inquire about it; the Pharisees had to hold a conclave over it; and though nearly nineteen centuries have slipped away, here are we at this hour meditating upon it. That man's opened eyes are enlightening ours today.[12]

Jesus heals the blind man by making use of the most prosaic possible means: dust and saliva, from which he makes a clay which he spreads over the man's eyes (v. 6). This is the essence of a sacrament: ordinary, secular things which become a sign and focus for the active presence of God. Jesus, who has just described himself as having been 'sent' by God (v. 4), now tells the man to 'go, wash in the pool of Siloam (which means Sent)': this is one nomad addressing another. The man does so and returns with his sight restored (v. 7). What is really striking in this passage is how Jesus sees, in both the blind man and the everyday phenomena of mud and spit, a potential, a new future, which no one else could have contemplated. Where we are prone to use the word 'restoration' to denote a careful reconstruction or recovery of the past – as in the heritage industry – Jesus shows no interest in restoring the past. His interest is in restoring the future. This itinerant, nomadic teacher and healer sees the future in people and things where everyone else is inclined to see only the past or the present.

The difference in approaches becomes apparent immediately the blind man is physically healed. He becomes a source and object, not of celebration but of inquisition: 'is this not the man who used to sit and beg?' ask some (v. 8). Those who had 'seen him before as a beggar' were unable, understandably enough perhaps, to see him now in the new humanity to which Jesus has restored him. One wonders how often we are similarly unable to see the potential, the subversive new future, that God longs to open up in those people – especially the very old, or the mentally ill, or the outsider – whom we can only see in the light of their past or present. Meanwhile, the man himself, pitched unexpectedly into this strange new world of sight and, even more, of *choice*, remains faithful to what has happened to him: he describes his healer as 'the man called Jesus', and when asked where Jesus is now replies, 'I do not know' (vv. 11–12). His journey, from blindness to sight, has only just begun, whilst others, as we now discover, are about to move in the opposite direction.

And it is at this point that, in a narrative *tour de force*, the evangelist opens up for us the contrast between two very different kinds of religion: the one inaugurated by Jesus, the nomad and outsider, and the other represented by the religious authorities in the story.[13] The contrast is drawn out in the central section of the story (vv. 13–34), in which Jesus is entirely absent, a point to which we shall return. Having entered the life of the blind man, and restored an almost unimaginable new future to him, he steps

19

back out of the way, allowing the man to choose for himself how to respond. So the religion of Jesus is world-centred: he encounters the man 'as he went along', at the roadside, the two nomads meeting one another. By contrast, the religion of the authorities is structure-centred: they only see the man, and Jesus, in terms of the problems both create for their religious rules (partly because Jesus had healed the man on the sabbath, and partly because the man himself refuses to accept that as a result Jesus must have been a sinner, vv. 14–17).

But there are more important differences between the two kinds of religion represented here. The religion of Jesus is not just world-centred but person-centred, where that of the authorities is rule-centred. The religion of Jesus is inclusive and proactive, whereas that of the authorities is exclusive and reactive: they accept only those people who conform to their rules, and they take no notice of a blind beggar until he is, so to speak, thrust upon them ('They brought to the [religious authorities] the man who had formerly been blind', v. 13). Jesus the nomad seeks people out: the religious authorities are immobile, invariably waiting for people to come to them. Even more important than this, the religion of Jesus represents the fulfilment of that process of creation we saw initiated in the opening chapter of Genesis: it is, in that rich sense of the word, creative, disturbing the status quo, drawing out new identity and meaning from (so to speak) the unfulfilled incompleteness of a blind roadside beggar whom no one notices. By contrast, the religion of the authorities neither creates nor disturbs: it *divides* ('And they were divided', v. 16). The religion of Jesus *attracts* people: although it is Jesus who first takes the initiative, the blind man responds to that initiative by freely embarking on a journey of discovery, about himself and about God, that draws him towards the central mystery of who Jesus is. By contrast, the religion of the authorities *terrifies* people: the blind man's parents are inhibited by fear of the authorities from telling them the truth about their son (v. 22). So the religion of Jesus is attentive, open to the possibilities that are latent in even the least likely people or places, whilst the religion of the authorities is closed, unresponsive ('I have told you already, and *you would not listen*', v. 27), unwilling to contemplate a God who operates outside their boundaries and rules.

But the final dimensions of the contrast are even more important still. As we have seen, the religion of Jesus judges people by where they are going, by all that they might be once the free gift of God's grace begins to work in their lives and they choose freely to respond. By contrast, the religion of the authorities judges people by where they have come from: 'we know that God has spoken to Moses,' declare the authorities with typically ecclesiastical grandiloquence, 'but as for this man, we do not know where he comes from' (v. 29). After all, he might not have gone to the right theological college or rabbinic seminary. *He might not be one of us.* Which brings us to the last and most important difference of all. The religion of Jesus is interested in *changing* people; the religion of the authorities is interested in *controlling* them: when they could not persuade the man to admit that Jesus must be a sinner, they 'drove him out' (v. 34), excluding him from his own faith community and leaving him entirely alone, and no doubt by this time beginning to wish he'd stayed blind.

And it is at this climactic moment in the story that Jesus reappears, the two nomads encountering one another for the second time. Jesus' long absence is no coincidence: partly it is, as we have seen, integral to the distinctiveness of what Jesus offers us, namely, a faith rooted in transformation and a new future but never in compulsion, a faith that always confers choice and freedom on the recipient. But partly Jesus' absence is a reflection by the evangelist on what it means to be a Christian nomad. Jesus enters our lives, encounters us in the midst of the everyday, and invites us to contemplate a future we had probably never considered possible, and certainly never taken seriously. In order to make that future our own we may, like the blind man, have to step out in faith and take action which will expose us to ridicule: imagine what passers-by would have said if they had seen the blind man, his face covered with a disgusting mixture of saliva and dirt, groping his way towards Siloam simply because a total stranger had told him he would be healed if he did so! And we may well discover, as he did, that much of our subsequent Christian pilgrimage feels anti-climactic, even severely testing, as we find ourselves pitched into an unfamiliar new world of choices and decisions in which Jesus appears conspicuous by his absence. The love of Jesus is no guarantee of a problem-free existence, or even of a constant

21

sense of his presence with us. Rather it takes the form of a disturbance, an unlooked-for annunciation in our lives, an invitation to a quite different way of seeing ourselves and the world. Remaining faithful to that invitation will be demanding and sometimes lonely, but those willing to take that risk will find a fellow-traveller who is not under our control, and yet who does not abandon us even though there are times when it feels as though he has.

We should notice, then, the kind of care and love that Jesus shows to the man: it is tender, personal, concerned with nurture in the fullest sense of that word – with wholeness, and growth, and both physical and spiritual well-being: Jesus touches the man, speaks to him, opens up for him new possibilities and horizons – *and then* steps back out of the way. He does not control the man: he loves him, and lets him go. But he doesn't give up on him either, even when the religious people do (and all too often religious people do just that, if the person stops coming or just doesn't fit into their systems). And when things go wrong for the man, Jesus is still there for him, still waiting to keep him company and take him further. Waiting characterizes much of the spirituality of both the nomad and the exile, as it did the life of both Jesus and the man born blind: waiting for conditions to change, or for others to act. Asylum seekers from poorer countries have usually spent most of their waking hours there working: the abrupt contrast to a state of helpless dependence and waiting can be overwhelming. This is the experience of a young Iraqi arriving in the UK:

> Stress-related illnesses, consequences of torture, angina – they often start once they get here. How much people change over five years! Limited choices, uncertainty. Your whole life is on hold when you're awaiting a decision. Access to adult education, you want to study, or work, but you can't focus or concentrate with the waiting . . .[14]

And yet it is precisely when the man born blind is most desperately in need, effectively disowned by his parents and explicitly excommunicated by the religious authorities, even more radically alone in the world than he was as a blind beggar, that he experiences this second encounter with his fellow nomad. Jesus, who has already seen the potential, the full possible identity, of the blind man, now invites the man to see his: 'Do you believe in the Son of

22

Man?' he asks him (v. 35). But the man does not yet see all that there is to see in Jesus, although he has already progressed far beyond the religious authorities, for whom Jesus is no more than a disruptive sinner and rule-breaker.[15] He has declared Jesus to be 'a prophet' (v. 17), and when challenged by the authorities to admit that Jesus is a sinner he comes out with this magnificent riposte:

'Here is an astonishing thing! You do not know where [Jesus] comes from, and yet he opened my eyes. We know that God does not listen to sinners, but he does listen to one who worships him and obeys his will. Never since the world began has it been heard that anyone opened the eyes of a person born blind. If this man were not from God, he could do nothing.' (vv. 30–3)

Yet he does not see the full truth about Jesus until Jesus himself gently points it out to him ('You have seen [the Son of Man], and the one speaking with you is he', v. 37). Here, at the end of the story, is the true miracle: the moment of recognition, in which the man born blind sees the fullness of the truth about Jesus, just as earlier Jesus had already seen a new future in him which no one else, perhaps not even the blind man himself, could have imagined. And the only proper response to the man's recognition of Jesus is worship: 'He said, "Lord, I believe." And he worshipped him' (v. 38). Worship is not just the recognition of the truth about God: it is the recognition of the truth about ourselves – that we are not created for autonomy, not made to cope with life on our own, even when – in fact, precisely when – we may be tempted to think we can. After all, the man born blind had been set free by Jesus to take control of his own life, only to discover that life as a free agent is neither as easy nor as attractive as it sounds. In offering Jesus his worship, he shows that he has accomplished a stage on his journey which all of us must make: he has moved from childish and helpless dependence on others to childlike and mature trust in God.

Even this, however, is not quite the end. As Jesus pronounces both the moral of the story and the heart of his mission ('I came into this world for judgment so that those who do not see may see, and those who do see may become blind', v. 39), it becomes apparent that the story is in effect a double pilgrimage: it describes the journey of the blind man from blindness to sight, and that of the religious authorities in the opposite direction. 'Surely we are not blind, are we?' ask the authorities of Jesus (v. 40). And Jesus replies, 'If you were blind, you would not have sin. But now that you say, "We see," your sin remains' (v. 41). Why? Because they do not see at all. They have no eyes for the blind beggar in their midst. They do not see the God at work in the street, outside their control. Or rather, they see both, but recognize neither. Not the least of the insights of this extraordinary story is the way it invites us to make our own a deeper way of seeing, a willingness to move from being spectators in life, surfing comfortably along its consumerist surface, to being participants, for whom really to see both God and our neighbour is to accept our need to be changed by both.

The story of the man born blind is a story about all of us; but it is a story of judgement as well as of encouragement. For if all of us are invited to make our own the journey of the blind man, we are also invited to consider how often we behave like the other characters in the story: the disciples, more at ease with talking *about* people in need rather than talking *to* them; the parents, unable or unwilling to put their heads above the parapet and risk offending people with power; or the religious authorities, whom it is easy to lampoon until we recall that every single feature of the religion they are described as representing has been enthusiastically practised by the Christian Church at one time or another during the past two thousand years.

And, by contrast, Jesus is the nomad, unconfined either by religious structures or by the human condition, for even death could not constrain him: 'He is not here,' said the young man in the empty tomb to the women who came looking for the dead Jesus. 'Go, tell his disciples and Peter that he is going ahead of you to Galilee' (Mark 16:6–7). The resurrection appearances only serve to underline what the Gospel accounts have already implied: that Jesus is elusive, apt to disappear just when we thought we understood him, always one step ahead of those who follow him, waiting for them to catch him up.

We have come a long way from the two drifters, off to see the world, in Mancini and Mercer's famous song. And yet there is a sense in which we have simply come full circle. The passionate

24

longing for a different kind of world that we saw in the spirituality of the *ger* and Psalm 119 is not so far away from 'the same rainbow's end' in 'Moon River': both speak to a condition of unfulfilment and incompleteness, a sense that there must be more to life than this. The pool of Siloam, in the story of the man born blind, is often understood to represent the waters of baptism[16] (though that makes sense only for as long as we see baptism not simply as admission into an ecclesiastical institution but as an invitation to accompany Jesus on the journey of a lifetime). But, like the waters of chaos at the dawn of time, or the great river, wider than a mile, that offers so much to those willing to travel with it, Siloam invites us into a different way of seeing the world around us, and ourselves too: seeing all that might be, not just all that is, seeing God's always surprising new future in the least likely people and places – and recognizing that we are ourselves, in some mysterious and yet fundamental way, 'sent', called out, like Abraham and Moses and Ruth, for a purpose and a journey. In such a context, 'Moon River', no less than Psalm 119 or the story of the man born blind, is an invitation to make that purpose and journey our own: 'Oh, dream maker, you heartbreaker, wherever you're going, I'm going your way.'

## CHAPTER THREE

# *California Dreamin'*

## *The Use of Memory and Stories in Exile*

This is the opening of a popular song from the 1960s, familiar from its recording by the American group The Mamas and the Papas:

> All the leaves are brown
> And the sky is grey,
> I've been for a walk
> On a winter's day.
> I'd be safe and warm
> If I was in L.A.
> > *California dreamin'*
> > *On such a winter's day.*

> Stopped into a church
> I passed along the way.
> Well, I got down on my knees
> And I pretend to pray.
> You know, the preacher likes the cold:
> He knows I'm gonna stay:
> > *California dreamin'*
> > *On such a winter's day . . .*

The song catches the mood prevailing among young Americans in the 1960s, of rootlessness and nostalgia. But it also catches an older American dream: the longing of poor travellers and would-be settlers to reach California, a land popularly believed to be as rich in milk and honey (and perhaps more enduring substances

26

too) as the promised land was for the children of Israel. That in turn only serves to remind us that neither rootlessness nor nostalgia are anything new. Here is another song that speaks of them:

> By the waters of Babylon we sat down and wept
> when we remembered Zion.
> As for our lyres, we hung them up
> on the willows that grow in that land.
> For there our captors asked for a song,
>     our tormentors called for mirth:
> "Sing us one of the songs of Zion."
> How shall we sing the Lord's song
> in a strange land?
> If I forget you, O Jerusalem,
> let my right hand forget its skill.
> Let my tongue cleave to the roof of my mouth
>     if I do not remember you,
> if I set not Jerusalem above my highest joy.
>
> Remember, O Lord, against the people of Edom
>     the day of Jerusalem,
> how they said, "Down with it, down with it,
>     even to the ground."
>
> O daughter of Babylon, doomed to destruction,
> happy the one who repays you
>     for all you have done to us;
>
> Who takes your little ones,
> and dashes them against the rock.

Few if any of the psalms are as explicit about their context as Psalm 137: none surpass it in the terrible virulence of its closing imprecation. Like 'California Dreamin'', Psalm 137 gives us vivid details of the place of exile: where the 1960s' song speaks of a cold autumnal bleakness, the psalmist describes the trees by the river-banks (or perhaps canals) of Babylon. And both songs introduce us to the painful paradox of memories during the experience of exile: they are indispensable, because they remind us of where we have come from, and of where, perhaps, we would one day love to be again; but they are agonizingly painful, for the very act of remembering

27

heightens the sense of dislocation, of not-belonging and of not being in control, which as we have seen is central to any experience of exile. The Jewish people have been there many times since the writing of this psalm: here is the experience of a group of Jewish prisoners in Chelmno, Poland, in 1942:

> After fifteen minutes the gendarme asked us to sing again. We tried to get out of it by pleading tiredness but to no avail. He ordered us to repeat after him: "We thank Adolf Hitler for everything!" We did so. Then we had to repeat, "We thank Adolf Hitler for our food." Then he demanded that we sing again. We sang the *Hatvikah*, and afterwards the twenty-sixth Psalm. (That was our response to the torment in our souls). Then he bolted the door again. We slept late into the night. I woke in the middle of the night probably from cold or nightmares. I began thinking everything over again. I wanted to scream: "Where is God in heaven? How can he see our torment and permit the slaughter of the innocent? Why doesn't he perform a miracle?"[1]

It is in this context that we should seek to make sense of Psalm 137's conclusion. This is not the prayer of the comfortable, but of the exile, the victim of the abuse of power. Experiences of this kind do not, generally, exalt or ennoble people: they brutalize them. It is easy for those who have never dwelt near anything resembling what the waters of Babylon meant for the Jews to criticize those who have. We should remember too that this closing verse is not, first and foremost, a threat, nor even a summons to action, but precisely a *prayer*, and we may hope that the ability to articulate our most destructive and negative feelings in our relationship with God may enable us, if not to let them go, at least to learn how to contain them. We shall return to this subject in the following chapter.

Anyone who has experienced any form of exile will know at first hand the paradoxical nature of memory that Psalm 137 explores. Your memory defines you, usually over against the Babylon in which you now find yourself: it gives you roots, identity, and therefore hope. But it also cruelly heightens your isolation, the often irrecoverable nature of what you have lost, and your inability to do anything about it. The memories may be idealized: *would* the singer of 'California Dreamin'' be 'safe and warm' if he or she

28

were in L.A.? We don't know, and sometimes, listening to an older person extolling the superiority of life in his or her youth, we may be tempted gently to dissent from so one-sided a presentation. And the memories of those in exile will in any case almost certainly be a discordant mix of pleasure and pain: a kind of bleak sadness at the irrecoverable pastness of some memories will be combined with a sharp sense of relief that other memories, of great trauma, are now safely distant. An Argentine woman in exile wrote that 'The effects of exile stay with you all your life. They are like things hidden in a closet. They suddenly jump out at you, like jack-in-the-box toys.'[2]

Yet, one-sided or not, the memories are uniquely precious, for they tell us who we are as well as where we have come from. Here, as so often, the Bible goes to the heart of the matter: the story of Eden, irrespective of how far one accepts any doctrine of 'original sin', presents a subtle blueprint of how life was intended to be, the shared memory that Adam and Eve and all their descendants carried with them into exile. But the memory is not simply of a paradisal garden where humans and creatures and plants could live together intimately with their Creator: it is also of distrust, insinuation, disobedience and the breakdown of relationships.

Yet perhaps above all it is a memory of *home*, however we understand that elusive term, which we take with us into exile. In Kenneth Grahame's timeless classic *The Wind in the Willows* there is a description of how the Mole, following the Rat through the wintry fields on a December evening, suddenly smells something familiar:

Home! That was what they meant, those caressing appeals, those soft touches wafted through the air, those invisible little hands pulling and tugging, all one way! Why, it must be quite close by him at that moment, his old home that he had hurriedly forsaken and never sought again, that day when he first found the river! And now it was sending out its scouts and its messengers to capture him and bring him in. Since his escape on that bright morning he had hardly given it a thought, so absorbed had he been in his new life, in all its pleasures, its surprises, its fresh and captivating experiences. Now, with a rush of old memories, how clearly it stood up before him, in the darkness! Shabby indeed, and small and poorly furnished, and yet his, the home he had made for himself, the home he had been so happy to get back to after his day's work. And the home had been happy with him, too, evidently, and was missing him, and wanted him back, and was telling him so, through his nose, sorrowfully, reproachfully, but with no bitterness or anger; only with plaintive reminder that it was there, and wanted him.[3]

The Mole was fortunate: he could go home, though for him too there could be no question of going *back* home. It was instead a journey of discovery, sensitively guided by the Rat, who (like a good spiritual director) helped the Mole to value afresh the modest but precious place he called home. Kenneth Grahame wrote out of a sure-footed awareness of the spiritual significance of place, and of land, as well as of the homing instinct in animals: in his study of animal migration, Matthieu Ricard tells the story of an experiment with cats:

Some cats were taken from a town and placed in darkened containers and then transported some miles away after a most complicated journey full of detours and retracing of steps. There was no possibility that the cats could use their memory of the route for this experiment. The cats were then taken from the containers and placed in the centre of a large maze with twenty-eight exits. The great majority of cats chose the exit that was in the direction of their home.[4]

The same remarkable instinct is found in many species of birds and mammals, as well as in fish (such as the salmon, which possesses the astonishing ability to retrace its steps to the place upriver where it was hatched, from somewhere in the midst of an ocean several years later). These journeys home are, so to speak, the creaturely equivalent of the journey of the Prodigal Son, who 'came to himself' in exile and made the decision to return to his father and brother, though here too it was a journey forward rather than a journey back, for both he and 'home' were profoundly changed by his earlier decision to leave.[5] The Hebrew tradition is remarkably consistent in this regard: hardly anyone in the Bible ever goes back home – and the way back to the primal home of Eden is in any case barred by 'a sword flaming and turning to

30

guard the way'.[6] Sarah and Abraham never return to Ur, and it is only the bones of Jacob and Joseph that return to the land of Canaan. Even Jesus rarely returns home to Nazareth, dying like Moses in exile, far from home. When he does go home, he can 'do no deed of power there'.[7] In part this is because the people of Nazareth, like the onlookers in the story of the man born blind, see Jesus in terms of his past ('Is not this the carpenter, the son of Mary . . . ?'):[8] as a result they are themselves blind with regard to who he might be, and to the new future to which he is calling them.

But there is another reason why the Bible is so consistent in its rejection of the notion of going *back* home. It contains no belief in the immortality (and hence the pre-existence) of the soul, a belief which led Plato to conclude that, for the good soul at least, death and the separation of soul from body allowed the soul to return to that eternal homeland from which it had come. Hence, epic Greek poetry like Homer's *Odyssey* could end with the hero returning home, even though here too both Odysseus and Ithaca were very different from when he first set out to Troy. The Judaeo-Christian tradition, rejecting any such notion, prefers to suggest that, in some sense or other, you could only go *forward* home, so to speak: the vision of the heavenly city with which the Bible closes is very different from that of the Garden of Eden with which it opens. The same thing is true in our own experience of exile: those who leave hospital, or prison, or any place of exile in order to return home rapidly discover that they are not, and cannot go, *back* home, for both they and 'home' are different from what they were when they first set out. Our memories of home both nourish and unsettle us: part of their power as well as their pain resides in the sharp spiritual truth that nostalgia is not an option. There is no way back.

This truth is powerfully explored in the prophetic writings of the Hebrew Bible. The prophet Jeremiah promises those exiled in Babylon that they will indeed return to their land and their homes, albeit after a long period in which they must settle in Babylon and seek the welfare of its people as well as their own.[9] But when they do return, God will do a new thing with and through them, creating a new covenant with them.[10] And in this new society, aliens will be given land as well, and foreigners will be

31

called by God to be priests and Levites.[11] This is no slack syncretism: in the books of Ezra and Nehemiah, the restoration of Jerusalem was accompanied by a stern insistence on keeping Israel's spiritual identity safe and distinctive in an increasingly multicultural society. But this too is no return to an imagined ideal past. Memory in exile, as we shall see, is always a spur to the envisioning of a new and different future.

None of this is to suggest that those in exile cannot or should not return if and when they are able to do so: it is simply to argue that any such return will always be a going *forward* home, not a going back. Within nine months of the ending of the Rwandan genocide, more than 750,000 former Tutsi exiles had moved back to Rwanda, including many who had never lived or even set foot there before. Why?

> The legacy of exclusion, the pressures of exile, and the memory of, or longing for, a homeland all played a part. So did a widespread determination to defy the genocide, to stand and be counted in a place where one was meant to have been wiped out.[12]

For those driven into exile in Babylon, memories of home inevitably brought with them searching reflection on the reasons why God appeared to have forsaken them. The prophet Jeremiah explores this issue directly in a vivid parable in which God shows him two baskets of figs, one very good and the other very bad: the former represented the mass of innocent exiles, victims of bad government and unfaithfulness to God, while the latter represented the royal elite around King Zedekiah who were responsible for the exile in the first place.[13] Their own spiritual response to the catastrophe of exile may find expression in Psalm 89: the first two-thirds of this extraordinary prayer appear to celebrate God's promise to be faithful to his covenant people, even quoting God's words back to him. As the crux approaches, the language becomes more explicit: this is what you promised us, Lord – that you would never forsake us, even if on occasions you deservedly punished us for our sins. Then comes the terrible indictment: yet you have done exactly what you promised not to do!

> You have broken the covenant with your servant,
> and have cast his crown to the dust . . .

32

All who pass by despoil him,
and he has become the scorn of his neighbours . . .
Remember how short my time is,
how frail you have made all mortal flesh.[14]

Here it is *God* whose memory appears to have lapsed, and who needs to be challenged to remember what has happened. It may not always be easy to sympathize with the plight of those who have been stripped of power and thrown into exile. But this psalm makes it possible for us to pray for all who are struggling to make some sense of what has happened to them: for the victims of ethnic cleansing, and for all who feel the God who once blessed and sustained them has inexplicably left them to their fate.

In any experience of exile, then, memory serves at least three fundamental purposes. First, it gives us a story, a past, an identity. We are more than a number in a prison wing, or a name scrawled above a bed in a hospital ward. Bureaucracies are inclined to forget this inconvenient individuality, preferring to deal with faceless forms and figures. Some regimes have even endeavoured to erase memories altogether, as the Soviet Empire famously tried to do by rewriting its own history without reference to dissidents. Mahnaz Afkhami, an Iranian woman and former cabinet minister forced into exile shortly before the fall of the Shah, writes:

You are told often [as an exile] that you must distance yourself from the past, that you must start a new life. But as in the case of death of kin – you don't want to move away, close his room, give away his clothes. You want to talk about him, look at pictures, exchange memories . . . You work frantically to retain the memory and to reconstruct the past . . . I sought mostly the company of other exiled Iranians. Together we listened to Persian stories, exchanged memories, recalled oft-repeated stories and anecdotes, and allowed ourselves inordinate sentimentality. We remembered tastes, smells, sounds. We knew that no fruit would ever have the pungent aroma and the luscious sweetness of the fruit in Iran, that the sun would never shine so bright, nor the moon shed such light as we experienced under the desert sky in Kerman . . .[15]

It is crucial for exiles of every description to hold firm to their stories and memories, and for those who encounter them to give those stories and memories their loving attention. The alternative is an easy stereotyping of those in exile, as well as a critical failure to value the stories and wisdom they carry with them. For the exile, holding onto memories is, however, neither easy nor comfortable, and not only because some of them are painful: a Burundian woman now living in England and seeking asylum told me of the agony of calling to mind her two children, whom she had been forced to leave behind without knowing what would happen to them. None the less, such memories remind you of who you are, and help to inoculate you against an unquestioning canonizing (or at least acceptance) of the present, and the status quo.[16] This is what Brian Keenan wrote about the importance of memories during his long incarceration as a hostage in Beirut:

> My father, who had died a few years before, was frequently in my thoughts. At first there were simple incidents from the family history. Certain moments seemed to become more complete and more filled with meaning. I seemed to understand more about each incident in the history than I did when the event occurred. These memories became less and less a recording of the past. My father became not just simply a memory but more a real presence; a presence I could feel more than see, a comforting reassurance that eased the hurt into a deeply filled sadness, yet that same sadness as it became reflective, lifted me. I began to understand the hurt that was in me. We are all creatures in need of love. My pity moved beyond myself. I wanted to reach out and embrace life. I thought of how those who have gone from us come back to us, a source of strength that fills us with warmth.[17]

And this brings us to the second reason why memory is so important in exile: because, so often, it defines people over against the prevailing power or system of control. When St Matthew opens his Gospel with a genealogy, he is doing far more than tracing Jesus' family tree: he is showing us how this Jesus, who is descended from a strange mixture of women and men, the powerless and the powerful, is also heir to a story which is framed by exiles: the first name is that of Abraham, sent out from home by God without knowing where he was going; the central names ('Jechoniah and his brothers') are explicitly linked with the

34

deportation to Babylon; and the last name, Joseph the husband of Mary, will have to make himself and his family into exiles to escape the wrath of Herod. This is no conventional pedigree for a conventional leader, but the subversive history of someone who will seek to turn the world upside down.

Finally, memory in exile serves to help us imagine and anticipate a new future. Nowhere is this clearer than in Psalm 77, where the psalmist struggles to make sense of a situation of great suffering ('the day of my trouble') by a conscious act of remembering 'your wonders of old time': this attentive meditation on the ways God was believed to have been active in the corporate memories of the psalmist's community offers no direct explanation of what is happening now; but it does implicitly challenge the present by using the past to point to a different future. This use of memory is not restricted to the Judaeo-Christian tradition: the classical Roman poet Ovid, exiled by the Emperor Augustus to an obscure Black Sea town, writes to the consul Graecinus in Rome, using his memory to imagine him: 'Yet will I use my mind, which alone is not exiled, to behold . . . you now dispensing justice to the people, and . . . being present at your decisions.' And he goes on to express the hope that his addressee might put in a word for him before the senate.[18] A much later Roman citizen, St Augustine of Hippo, gave the classical understanding of memory Christian clothing in his *Confessions*:

> There [in my memory] I meet myself and recall what I am, what I have done, and when and where and how I was affected when I did it. There is everything that I remember, whether I experienced it directly or believed the word of others. Out of the same abundance in store, I combine with past events images of various things, whether experienced directly or believed on the basis of what I have experienced; and on this basis I reason about future actions and events and hopes, and again think of all these things in the present. 'I shall do this and that', I say to myself within that vast recess of my mind which is full of many, rich images, and this act or that follows. 'O that this or that were so,' 'May God avert this or that.'[19]

In his *The Trinity*, Augustine connects memory with worship, for the latter recalls to mind the soul's capacity for God and for participation in God.[20] For Christians this connection is crucial: when we break bread in obedience to Christ's command, we are remembering the story of his last meal with his disciples and his crucifixion, not in order to return to it, but in order to re-present it now, so that it becomes a prophetic reminder that we are made for more than exile, and that we take our past with us into the creating of a new future. Imprisoned by the Nazis in the concentration camp at Terezín, near Prague, eleven-year-old Ivo Katz wrote this poem:

Some day we shall outrun this hour,
Some day there will be comfort for us,
And hope again burst into flower,
And peace and guardian care restore us.
The jug of tears will break and spill,
And death be ordered, "Hush, be still!"

The true dawn will come at last,
Wine from water be revealed,
Some day all our tears be past,
Some day all our wounds be healed.
All our slavish chains, some day,
God will smite and strike away . . .

Some day all sorrows will take flight,
This life thus wretched and laborious.
The saviour will appear in might,
With his all-conquering power victorious.
Some day, if God will, we'll stand
Free men in the promised land.

Some day the aloes will bloom fair,
Some day the palms bear fruit again,
Some day the burden of despair
Be lifted to assuage our pain.
And in God's house we'll live anew.
Some day all these things will be true![21]

Ivo did not live to see this new future: he died at Terezín on 18 December 1943, aged eleven and a half. And it is no easy matter to use one's memories to envisage a new future in this way, either for those like Ivo who have had their future taken from them, or for all who through the experience of ageing enter a new kind of exile: the loss of control and independence, and of the 'homeland' of childhood and youth. When my mother was approaching the end of her life, with a failing heart and a proneness to depression, she would often say, 'I wish God would take me. I'm no use to anyone.' I wish I had had the wisdom to reply with the words that Metropolitan Anthony of Sourozh used when his grandmother made a similar remark to him about her sense of uselessness: 'Since the world began and until eternity unfolds before us, no-one else was capable of being my grandmother.'[22] Even when advanced age strips us of the capacity to *do* something useful, we can still *be* uniquely ourselves, uniquely precious in the relationships we have spent a lifetime creating. And our memories, however fragmented and fitfully recalled, allow us to face even the bleakest future with hope, for they remind us that we are more than the sum of our biological parts, since our identities are constantly being recreated in and through the relationships that make us who we are – and above all in our perception, however doubtful and incoherent, of being loved by one in whom both our past and our future are forever present. This is the prayer of the elderly writer of Psalm 71, whose primal memory of the God who like a midwife brought her or him to birth still helps to point to a hopeful future:

> Upon you have I leaned from my birth,
> when you drew me from my mother's womb;
> my praise shall be always of you.
> I have become a portent to many,
> but you are my refuge and my strength . . .
> Do not cast me away in the time of old age;
> forsake me not when my strength fails . . .
> Forsake me not, O God, when I am old and grey-headed,
> till I make known your deeds to the next generation
> and your power to all that are to come . . .
> What troubles and adversities you have shown me,
> and yet you will turn and refresh me
> and bring me from the deep of the earth again.[23]

This is not nostalgia, but the defiant use of our past to help nurture our future. It is exactly this understanding of memory that underpins the Christian eucharist – the re-presenting of Jesus' last meal with his disciples in such a way that remembering his death, for us and in our place, sets us free from the fear of our own worthlessness to receive the free gift of God's new life. In such a context, even our 'California dreamin'' and our painful memories of the waters of Babylon can be transmuted into the raw material of a new future.

CHAPTER FOUR

# *This Nearly was Mine*
## *The Prayer of Lament in Exile*

Towards the end of Rodgers and Hammerstein's classic musical *South Pacific*, the French settler Emile sings 'This Nearly was Mine', a melancholy reflection on the failure of his relationship with the young American Nellie, who has told him she cannot marry him.

> One dream in my heart
> One love to be living for
> This nearly was mine.
> One girl for my dreams,
> One wonder in paradise,
> This promise of paradise,
> This nearly was mine.
> Close to my life she came,
> Only to fly away,
> Only to fly as day flies from moonlight.
> Now, now I'm alone,
> Still dreaming of paradise,
> Still saying that paradise
> Once nearly was mine . . .

The countless millions who have heard what is arguably the most famous musical ever written will not need reminding that it has a happy ending, at least in part: Emile and Nellie survive the war, and are reunited as the curtain falls. Other characters in the story do not survive, however, and, happy ending or not, 'This Nearly was Mine' can still evoke a response from all who have known the same sense of bleak and bitter disappointment, loss and hurt at the

39

failure of a relationship which had promised so much. And yet Emile's song has more in it than the articulation of what might have been: he is 'still dreaming of paradise', and not only through nostalgia: Edward Said has pointed out that the exile, precisely by having been uprooted and forced into a different world, is capable of envisaging other such worlds, able to 'dream of paradise' with an intensity and clarity unknown to those whose settled stability and sense of belonging have never been seriously challenged.[1]

In order to do that, however, the exile must first come to terms with the present, and one way to do that is through lament. In the language of spirituality, lament might be described as the way you respond when faith and experience collide painfully with one another. It is supremely the prayer of the powerless, of those not in control of what is happening to them. And it is closely linked to memory. Exiles cannot take with them their land, or their temples. But they can take their memories – not only their own experiences, but remembered texts that can nourish and sustain them in a strange land. Hence the importance of the almost-lost arts of rumination and recollection: the twin abilities both to bring consciously back to mind and heart, and digest thoroughly, all that you have experienced, and also to learn by heart and store safely in the memory texts that may sustain you 'by the waters of Babylon', or when, as in Emile's case, paradise seems to have passed you by. Both rumination and recollection make possible lament – the willingness to 'give sorrow words', as Shakespeare put it in *Macbeth*[2] – which can take the form either of a reflection *de novo* on what has happened, or of a recitation of a remembered text, or of both together. It need not be restricted to words, as we shall see, and it can embrace a wide variety of forms.

Here, to begin with, is one of the simplest:

How long will you forget me, O Lord; for ever?
How long will you hide your face from me?
How long shall I have anguish in my soul and grief in my
    heart, day after day?
How long shall my enemy triumph over me?

Look upon me and answer, O Lord my God;
lighten my eyes, lest I sleep in death;

40

Lest my enemy say, 'I have prevailed against him,'
and my foes rejoice that I have fallen.

But I put my trust in your steadfast love;
my heart will rejoice in your salvation.
I will sing to the Lord,
for he has dealt so bountifully with me. (Ps. 13)

Psalm 13 embodies a number of the classic features of the biblical lament, even within its short compass. Notice the fourfold repetition of the question 'how long?' The presence of question marks is one of the most important characteristics of the prayer of lament, and their absence from many otherwise comprehensive collections of prayers constitutes a grave impoverishment. Forms of prayer that do not allow room for questions imply a relationship with God in which there is no room for doubt or puzzlement, a point to which we shall return. And the fourfold repetition here is also significant, for as so often in the Hebrew Bible the repetition acts as an intensifier, hammering home the point in the same way as the repeated 'My God, my God' at the beginning of Psalm 22.

In the first section of the text, the writer of Psalm 13 articulates sharply the dislocation he or she is experiencing – the sense of puzzlement and outrage at being abandoned by God, the intensity of present suffering, and the awareness of being surrounded by hostile forces who are in control of what is happening. In the second section, the writer turns this articulation into prayer, and prayer of a very particular kind. The writer needs to know that God *sees* what is happening, for it *feels* as though God has hidden God's face – a common image in laments. More than that, though, the writer needs to *hear God's answer* to his or her repeated questions, for if there is no answer and no available source of explanation or meaning for what is happening, then the hostile forces have indeed triumphed. It is also worth noting, in this second section of Psalm 13, how the psalmist puts into direct speech the kind of thing those forces might be expected to say ('I have prevailed against him'): there is an earthy and resolute specificity about Hebrew prayer which is often lacking in the generalized blandness of its later Christian equivalents, which can too easily settle for an undemanding prayer for 'the oppressed' or 'the vulnerable' or 'the marginalized' without any robust sense of what it feels like to belong to these groups, or exactly what it is that they are up against.

The closing section of Psalm 13 reflects an abrupt change of tone: from despair to hope, from questions to confidence, from present to future, from lament to praise. This change occurs in many, though not all, biblical prayers of lament, and it can at first read as though someone has tacked a happy ending onto an otherwise gloomy text, as though religious people were not supposed to get depressed or live with questions. The abruptness of the change, however, is more apparent than real. It is *because* the psalmist has felt free to articulate his or her most urgent and honest questions, and then transmute them into prayer, that he or she can then begin to contemplate a different possible future. Praise, in prayers of lament, is not a naive optimism, but the defiant refusal to accept the seeming inevitability of what is happening, and the determined willingness to lift God's future into the present and to celebrate it even when there is no sign whatever of it coming to pass.[3] It is very significant that in some of the great psalms of lament (such as Psalms 22, 69 or 102) a further change is evident in the course of the prayer: from a narrowly focused preoccupation with the self at the beginning, to a much wider corporate context at the end. So Psalm 22 begins:

My God, my God, why have you forsaken me,
and are so far from my salvation, from the words of my
    distress?
O my God, I cry in the daytime, but you do not answer . . .

and ends:

I will tell of your name to my people;
in the midst of the congregation will I praise you . . .
They [future generations] shall come and make known his
    salvation,
to a people yet unborn,
declaring that he, the Lord, has done it.

As in any experience of exile, such as bereavement, you have to begin your praying where you are, for you cannot begin anywhere else. So you start with as honest as possible an articulation of what you are going through now, using language and imagery that

42

comes closest to capturing your meaning, and only as you work through this kind of praying can you even begin to envisage a wider, more corporate, more hopeful future. Just as Emile continues to dream of paradise even when it appears to have deserted him for ever, so the psalmist is in a position to glimpse other possibilities only after having struggled to make some sense of what is happening now.

Individual laments of this kind are common in the Hebrew Bible, the greatest of all being the extraordinarily sustained and moving exploration of innocent and inexplicable suffering in the Book of Job. Not all such laments are concerned with the plight of the individual who is praying. Thus, the short Book of Habakkuk is the prayer of someone who cannot understand why good people are being afflicted by enemies ('Why do you make me see wrong-doing and look at trouble?', 1:3), and wants to know what God is going to do about it. When the initial answer he appears to receive fails to satisfy him (since it appears to be God who is sending the enemies to wreak their havoc on his own people), he declares his intention to 'stand at [his] watch-post' (2:1) and, so to speak, to hang on in there until he gets a better answer. It is just this kind of persistent, stubbornly determined prayer which Jesus commends to his followers, most obviously in the story of the importunate widow and the unjust judge,[4] and in the end it bears fruit. Habakkuk is promised a real answer, even though he will still have to wait for it (2:3); yet his waiting has now been transformed from the passionate anger of his opening prayer to something far more hopeful, and his little book closes with precisely that subversive praise that refuses to collude in the unjust status quo and looks forward to God's new future:

> Though the fig tree does not blossom,
> and no fruit is on the vines;
> though the produce of the olive fails
> and the fields yield no food;
> though the flock is cut off from the fold
> and there is no herd in the stalls,
> yet I will rejoice in the Lord;
> I will exult in the God of my salvation. (3:17–18)

Not all laments are the prayers of individuals. Towards the end of the Book of Isaiah there is a magnificent communal lament (63:7–64:12), whose context may well be the profound sense of anticlimax and disappointment which characterized the spirituality of those who did in the end return from exile in Babylon, only to find life in their ancestral homeland to be very different from what they had anticipated.[5] It depicts God as a loving and tender parent who is rejected by his child and who thus becomes an enemy (63:10). This is a careful and honest piece of ruminating on past experience, rooted in the reiterated question 'Where [is God]?' (63:11, 15), with the directness of the hurt child calling for its parent ('Are your deepest feelings, your mercy to me, to be restrained? After all, you are our Father', 63:15–16 NJB). The prayer moves from asking God to '*look* down' (63:15) to asking God to '*come* down' (64:1): the logic of despair, as well as of love, is incarnation. And God answers by arguing that it is human failure to call upon him, not divine indifference, which has caused this new dislocation between God and humanity:

> I was ready to be sought out by those who did not ask,
>   to be found by those who did not seek me.
> I said, 'Here I am, here I am',
>   to a nation that did not call on my name.
> I held out my hands all day long
>   to a rebellious people,
> who walk in a way that is not good,
>   following their own devices . . . (65:1–2)

Yet, despite this bitter disappointment on God's part, God has not rejected the people, and the Book of Isaiah closes with an extraordinary envisioning of nothing less than a new cosmos ('I am about to create new heavens and a new earth', 65:17), with Jerusalem as its symbolic focus (65:18–19). Within this new cosmos, people will live to a ripe old age; lives will not be cut short; people will dwell in their own houses and enjoy the fruit of their own vineyards, 'for like the days of a tree shall the days of my people be' (65:22). Work will be fruitful, and the birth of children a joy. This is precisely a restoration of Eden; but it is a new Eden, not the old one brought back to life – as with Jesus' restoration of the blind man's sight in John 9, it is the restoration of a new future, not of a supposedly ideal past, that is in view. The animal creation will live together in peace, and there will be no more suffering or destruction (65:25). And the God who will do these things needs no religious sanctuary:

> Thus says the Lord:
> Heaven is my throne,
>     and the earth is my footstool;
> what is the house that you would build for me,
>     and what is my resting-place? (66:1)

The presence of God is not restricted to holy buildings. And those who seek to be fellow workers with God in the building of this new cosmos must resist the temptation fatally to narrow the cosmic divine vision and purpose to an arid religious perspective (66:3–4). Liturgy must breathe the divine justice, and reflect the cosmic scope of the divine purposes. The kind of person this God favours is 'the humble and contrite in spirit who trembles at my word' (66:2): this God is a mother who comforts and restores her people (66:13), promising them both physical and spiritual fulfilment (66:14), and judging their enemies (66:15–16).[6] This God will miraculously bring to birth a new nation against all expectations (66:7–9), and in this new nation priests and Levites will be drawn from all peoples, not just from Israel (66:21). This new nation will be prepared for by the sending of 'survivors' (effectively missionaries) (66:19) who will 'declare my glory among the nations'.

This tremendous vision anticipates not only Jesus' vision of the Kingdom but the sending out of the disciples 'to all the world' (Matt. 28), and the book closes with a universal prospect of all nations coming to Jerusalem to worship the Lord:

> From new moon to new moon,
>     and from sabbath to sabbath,
> all flesh shall come to worship before me,
>     says the Lord. (66:23)[7]

This double dynamic is striking: just as the 'survivors', those who have not only lived through the exile but also through the upheavals that will follow it, become ambassadors for this new cosmos, going out to make it known, so people from all nations will stream to the renewed Jerusalem so that it indeed becomes a symbol of universal restoration. Even more striking, though, is the

45

role played by the former exiles, who become redemptive figures, priests, who will help God bring this new creation to birth – just as Job becomes a redemptive figure when, at the end of his suffering, God restores a new future to him after he has prayed for his friends (Job 42:7–9).[8] We are encountering here perhaps the greatest paradox presented to us by the Bible's reflections on exile: that, while exile itself remains a deeply destructive experience, God is capable of transforming it into an opportunity for the unprecedented envisioning of a new and quite different future – not only for the exiles, but for all creation.[9]

One last biblical example of lament needs attention, and that is the most famous of all: the Book of Lamentations, formerly attributed to the prophet Jeremiah, and consisting of five laments (corresponding to the chapters), possibly all written for use as public laments of fasting and mourning in memory of the destruction of the Temple by the Babylonians in 587 BCE. Unlike the prophetic laments, these are all communal laments by the people themselves, expressive of genuine grief. They represent the prayer of lament in its most fundamental, pared-down form: they are the prayers of a people struggling, not just to find meaning in unimaginable affliction, but simply to *survive*: to describe what has happened, in the hope that the very act of description will help those who have lived through it to make some sense of what is left of their lives, and to look for witnesses – to seek to draw others (above all, God) into the mystery of this catastrophe, and thereby to make them participants, not simply distant spectators, in the struggle to come to terms with it. Like the terrible eighty-eighth Psalm, the Book of Lamentations offers no answers, from God or anyone else: as Tod Linafelt has recently suggested, 'the horizon of Lamentations, while *demanding* survival, was unable to *imagine* survival as a live option.'[10] Sometimes others must do that for you, giving the text an interpretative afterlife in their own experience, and perhaps it is only in this way that we may on occasions be able to align our own journeys through exile alongside those who have journeyed before us and will journey after us, making of our shared experience a source of some kind of meaning and hope in the shadow of the cross. In its moving evocations of almost unspeakable suffering, Lamentations may still articulate some of the horrors our world has witnessed since it was written:

46

The hands of compassionate women
   have boiled their own children;
they became their food
   in the destruction of my people . . .

Remember, O Lord, what has befallen us;
   look, and see our disgrace!
Our inheritance has been turned over to strangers,
   our homes to aliens.
We have become orphans, fatherless;
   our mothers are like widows.
We must pay for the water we drink;
   the wood we get must be bought . . .

You have wrapped yourself with anger and pursued us,
   killing without pity;
you have wrapped yourself with a cloud
   so that no prayer can pass through.[11]

Why is lament so important? Three answers at least may be suggested: theological, psychological, and political. Theologically, the prayer of lament may be seen in the light of the opening chapter of Genesis and the reflections made on it in the first chapter of this book. For the ancient Israelites, the belief in a God who created out of a chaos that was imaged as watery darkness made it natural to see exile, or any form of intense suffering, as precisely a reversal of that creative process, a return to the chaos from which they had been drawn. So the prayers of lament frequently use the nightmarish imagery of drowning to articulate what those who write or sing these prayers feel is happening:

Save me, O God,
   for the waters have come up, even to my neck.
I sink in deep mire where there is no foothold;
   I have come into deep waters and the flood sweeps over me.[12]

In this way lament may enable God to draw meaning and purpose even from the uttermost depths of despair, precisely by articulating those depths in prayer. It is true that biblical writers had a very different conception of the way God works from what we are likely to have today, lacking for the most part any theory of

47

secondary causes and assuming that almost everything that happened to them, whether good or bad, was the direct result of God's immediate action and intention. Yet this in no way invalidates the continuing relevance of their methods of praying, for it led them to the conviction that God was somehow involved in everything that happened, and that they had a right to question and challenge God when things went wrong.

But this right to challenge God derives from a much deeper theological truth, which underpins both the theory and the practice of the prayer of lament in Scripture: the nature of the covenant which the people of Israel believed God had made with them. We need not explore here the nature of the different covenants to be found in the Hebrew Bible, from that made with Noah and signed by the rainbow in the sky to the covenants with Abraham and Moses, the new covenants described by Jeremiah and Ezekiel and the covenant believed by Christians to have been sealed with the blood of Jesus.[13] What matters is the profound and pervasive sense, found throughout the Bible, that the people of God enjoyed a particular kind of relationship with their Creator, a relationship of love and trust and mutual faithfulness. This in turn gave them both the right and the confidence to cry out bitterly when God appeared to have rejected them – or when people began to behave as though there were no god at all.

> Why stand so far off, O Lord?
> Why hide yourself in time of trouble? . . .
> The wicked in their arrogance say, "God will not avenge it";
> In all their scheming God counts for nothing . . .
> They say in their heart, "God has forgotten;
> he hides his face; he will never see it."[14]

It is the existence of this relationship that inspires the person lamenting to an unprecedented boldness before God, demanding to know why God has bothered to create people at all in view of what happens to them, or insisting that God stop slumbering uselessly and wake up before it is too late, even on one occasion describing God as awakening belatedly out of sleep 'like a warrior who had been overcome with wine'.[15] This boldness introduces us to the second, psychological reason why lament matters, supremely in places and experiences of exile: because it reminds us

48

of our primal status not only as *creatures* of a loving Creator but as *children* of a loving parent – and, as such, with an inborn right to challenge and question that parent when faith and experience collide painfully with one another. In the Hebrew Bible this deep psychological awareness of being loved by God is, as we have seen, rooted in the notion of covenant; in the New Testament, it is explicit in the teaching of both St Paul and Jesus himself.[16]

Not everyone finds it easy to believe that they are personally and unconditionally loved, especially if they did not experience that love from their own parents. Psychiatrists like D.W. Winnicott and Anthony Storr have pointed out that children who believe, rightly or wrongly, that their parents' love for them is either non-existent or conditional upon their conforming to whatever was expected of them, will become excessively compliant, apt to say and do only what they think their parents will approve of, and repressing everything else. Winnicott wrote: 'The main thing to point out to people about infants and children is that life for infants and children is not easy even if it has all sorts of good things about it, and there is no such thing as life without tears, except where there is compliance without spontaneity.'[17] Elsewhere he wrote, 'Compliance carries with it a sense of futility for the individual and is associated with the idea that nothing matters and that life is not worth living', even though they may have had tantalizing glimpses of creative living.[18] And Anthony Storr adds:

> A child who shows this kind of partial compliance [as a result of feeling that his or her parents' love is conditional on good behaviour] is clearly not going to incorporate the inner sense of his own worth which develops in children who are certain that their parents' love for them will be unconditionally continued. Confidence that one is of value and significance as a unique individual is one of the most precious possessions which anyone can have.[19]

The belief that you are loved unconditionally gives you more than confidence: it gives you the freedom to be alone and yet trust that you have not been rejected, by your parents or those closest to you.[20] It also gives you the freedom to doubt and to ask questions. Above all, it gives you the freedom to fail: to know you will

49

still be loved and valued even if you make a terrible mess of your life. These freedoms, and the fundamental belief in unconditional love that underlies them, are the bedrocks of the biblical prayer of lament: they are what make it possible, and it is precisely when they are threatened or appear to have been withdrawn – in other words, it is precisely when the person is experiencing some form of exile – that lament becomes necessary. Only in and through lament can you try to articulate the questions that impose themselves upon you (Why is this happening to me? How could he, or she, or they, do such things to me? Where is God in all this?), and try, too, to rediscover something of that sense of trust without which creative (as distinct from compliant) living is impossible.[21] The person who believes that such questions cannot be asked of God does not really believe that God's love is unconditional: hence a form of spirituality or liturgy that cannot find space for lament is implicitly modelling an understanding of God that is alien to the Bible. Conversely, to bring your pain into your prayer is in itself an act of witness, even if the faith that underlies that act is at that very moment being stretched to breaking point – a testimony to the conviction that *what is happening is not right*, and that the God who created and goes on creating all things will not in the final analysis allow it to stand.

And this brings us to the third reason for the importance of the prayer of lament, which is its political significance. No one has expressed this with more power than Walter Brueggemann:

> A community of faith which negates laments soon concludes that the hard issues of justice are improper questions to pose at the throne [of God], because the throne seems to be only a place of praise. I believe it thus follows that if justice questions are improper questions at the throne (which is a conclusion drawn through liturgic use), they soon appear to be improper questions in public places, in schools, in hospitals, with the government, and eventually even in the courts. Justice questions disappear into civility and docility. The order of the day comes to seem absolute, beyond question, and we are left with only grim obedience and eventually despair. The point of access for serious change has been forfeited when the propriety of this speech form is denied.[22]

50

This is why it is essential for churches to find space for some form of lament in public worship on occasions when 'the hard issues of justice' are particularly topical – when an unjust war is being waged, unjust legislation being framed, or an easy populism being used to justify a narrow xenophobia in dealing with refugees and asylum seekers. It is also why we must hesitate before rushing to condemn the many references to 'enemies' in the biblical prayers of lament: these are texts which have arisen out of encounters with real and immediate evil, and if (as we saw earlier in Psalm 137) the person praying does not always measure his or her language, that only serves to remind us of the extent to which suffering and injustice disfigure and dehumanize people. We do not need either to condone or to criticize these violent prayers (especially if we are doing so from a safe and comfortable distance) in order to be able to offer them as imaginative intercession for those many exiles in our world to whom these ancient prayers may still offer a voice. Indeed, using them in this way allows our intercession to extend our sense of kinship: to enlarge the boundaries of our compassion, and to pray in a much more informed (because more *imaginative*) way for those who suffer as the psalmist once did.

It is against this rich theological, psychological and political background that we may best understand the prayers of lament, and consider how to appropriate them for our own day. It is this background which may help us to understand, for example, the striking relationship within these prayers of protest and intimacy: thus, Psalm 73 moves from a vigorous subversion of traditional religious orthodoxy about the supposed fate of the wicked to a profound and personal expression of childlike trust in God. The pivot of the psalm is the point at which the psalmist takes his or her rage and puzzlement at the seeming triumph of the wicked *into the sanctuary*: by making space, in our worship and our church buildings, for the articulation of these most difficult questions we also allow people to move from doubt and distress to intimacy and back again, in exactly the way that children who believe themselves to be unconditionally loved can switch quite unaffectedly from rage to trusting intimacy in their relationship with their parents. In a similar way, Jesus' own lament over Jerusalem oscillates between fierce anger and an intimate maternal love, and back again.[23] More recently, Nicholas Wolterstorff, whose 25–year-old son was killed in a mountaineering accident, wrote 'every lament is a love-song. Will love-songs one day no longer be laments?'[24]

These apparently violent and artificial changes of mood within the prayers of lament also only make sense against the background sketched above. One of the greatest of them all, Psalm 102, begins (as we have seen) in a narrowly individual context:

> O Lord, hear my prayer:
> and let my crying come before you.

It ends in a resolutely corporate one:

> The children of your servants shall continue,
> and their descendants shall be established in your sight.

In between, however, the prayer encompasses a wide range of moods and thoughts, from utter despair to surging hope and back again. For reasons already given, this should not surprise us: it is surely the sign of a healthy relationship to be able to accommodate every conceivable change of mood and subject, as well as characteristic of most people struggling to make some sense of, say, bereavement or desolation. Two other features of this (and of many other) such prayers are worth noting. The first is the striking use of imagery: smoke, a furnace, grass, birds, shadows, items of clothing are all drawn in to help the psalmist describe his or her predicament. Almost all the imagery of these prayers is drawn from secular life, and some of them have particular overtones which can help us grasp the power of the image in question. Thus this psalmist says,

> I am become like a vulture in the wilderness,
> like an owl that haunts the ruins. (Ps. 102:7)

To a modern reader, this image may simply evoke a sense of utter desolation. But the original writer will have known that owls were among the species categorized as unclean in the *torah*.[25] This is an evocation, not just of loneliness, but of social rejection – the prayer of a leper, and today, perhaps, of the victim of AIDS. Images can, of course, be interpreted in many ways – hence their poetic power – and we may allow them to speak to us as they will. Above all, though, images allow us to articulate those parts of our

52

experiences which concepts and flat prose could never reach, enabling us both to get in touch with what is happening to us and then to move on.

The second striking feature of Psalm 102 is the way the psalmist moves seamlessly from talking *to* God to talking *about* God, from prayer to theology, and back again. This too needs to be understood against the background sketched above. For the people who wrote or first sung these prayers, there was no dividing-line between attentive devotion and vigorous theological reflection: indeed each informed and stretched the other. The psalmist, here as so often, sets his or her own personal experience in the context of the common faith of the people of God, and this psalm concludes with a magnificent synthesis of both: the psalmist's *prayer* is deepened and enlarged by being set against a wider background of the shared faith of the people, whilst the psalmist's *theology* or faith is changed by virtue of its collision, so to speak, with present experience – the psalmist comes to see that human limitation and mortality are in fact part of the essential condition of all creation, even including the heavens:

> [God] has brought down my strength in my journey
> and has shortened my days.
> I pray, "O my God, do not take me in the midst of my days;
> your years endure throughout all generations.
>
> "In the beginning you laid the foundations of the earth,
> and the heavens are the work of your hands;
>
> "They shall perish, but you will endure;
> they all shall wear out like a garment.
>
> "You change them like clothing, and they shall be changed;
> but you are the same, and your years will not fail.
>
> "The children of your servants shall continue,
> and their descendants shall be established in your sight."
> (vv. 24–9)

Lament has not always been given the significance it deserves in Christian liturgy and spirituality, doubtless because it has often suited those in authority in both Church and State to encourage those in any kind of exile to accept their condition meekly rather than to challenge or question it.[26] But there are some fascinating examples of its appearance, often on the fringes of what is officially approved. There is evidence of medieval Christians engaging in a liturgical denunciation of the local saint, sometimes known as the *clamor*, when they believed that their prayer had not been answered: psalms of lament might be sung at one of the holiest points of the Mass, between the 'but deliver us from evil' and the 'Amen' of the Our Father, after which the relics of the saint would be 'humiliated' by being set on the floor alongside the worshippers. Sometimes people went further: there are records of peasants at Saint-Calais-sur-Anille who, having been wronged by a local lord, entered the parish church late at night:

> First, they lay before the altar praying and crying. Then they rose and two of the peasants stood on either side of the altar, removed the altar cloths, and then began to strike the altar stone containing relics of St Calais all the while *clamantes*: "Why don't you defend us, most holy lord? Why do you ignore us, sleeping so? Why don't you free us, your slaves, from our great enemy?" etc. The guards heard the commotion and came running to the altar. On seeing what was happening, they expelled the peasants from the church. Needless to say, a short time later the evil noble fell from his horse and broke his neck . . . [27]

The prayer of lament need not, of course, be offered only, or even at all, in the form of words: it can be danced, painted, or turned into music – the great majority of the biblical prayers of this kind were, after all, undoubtedly intended to be sung. Many such musical examples now exist, by no means all of them recent, and there is space to mention only a few.

The French composer Jehan Alain (1911–40) was killed in action aged twenty-nine, just five days before France's surrender during the Second World War. His instructions about how his famously tempestuous organ piece *Litanies* (1937) should be performed are instructive:

> You must create an impression of passionate incantation. Prayer is not a lament but a devastating tornado, flattening everything in its way. It is also an obsession. You must fill men's ears with it, and God's ears too! If you get to the end without feeling

exhausted you have neither understood it nor played it as I would want it.

The score itself is headed with a quotation which can be related to the death of one of Alain's sisters in 1937:

When the Christian soul is in distress and cannot find any fresh words to implore God's mercy, it repeats the same prayer unceasingly with overwhelming faith. The limit of reason is past. It is faith alone which propels its ascent.[28]

The Scottish Catholic composer James MacMillan has, in his *Cantos Sagrados* (1989), set poems by Ariel Dorfman and others (including an extraordinarily moving lament to Our Lady of Guadalupe by Ana María Mendoza), which allow both the suffering and the hard questions of bereaved mothers in Argentina, whose children had been victims of government repression, to find expression. His *Tuireadh* (Gaelic for 'lament'), written in 1991 for clarinet and string quartet, was MacMillan's response to the explosion on the North Sea oil-rig Piper Alpha, and evokes in purely musical terms the 'keening' which forms part of the traditional response of mourners, especially women, to intense grief, and which is found in the Bible: the prophet Jeremiah declares the words of God:

Consider, and call for the mourning women to come;
   send for the skilled women to come;
let them quickly raise a dirge over us,
   so that our eyes may run down with tears . . . [29]

Such music need not be explicitly religious to contain a powerful spiritual charge. The Swedish composer Allan Pettersson (1911–80) was born and raised in conditions of poverty and violence, with a father who was an alcoholic, in the Stockholm suburb of Södermalm. He sought in his music to combine a sense of outrage at the sufferings he had witnessed in his own life with a similar protest at the structures of injustice and inequality he saw in the world as a whole. In one of his haunting *Barefoot Songs* he reflected on his own life:

Mother is poor and the pot sits empty,
and the cold is piercing and howls.

The boy is thin and squints,
and he arches his back like a cat.
Father is in good spirits with his schnapps;
he talks about stars and planets.
Yes, the Lord God has no interest
in the star that is called Earth.[30]

In 1958, in an interview to mark the premiere of his Third Concerto for String Orchestra, he said:

It is mother who *is* my music. It is her voice that speaks in it, I've wanted to cry out what she could never say, she and my sister, my sister who never got to be a woman, who was stunted by rheumatoid arthritis, who nearly threw herself out of the window because of the pain and who died one Christmas Eve in the Söder Hospital.[31]

A few years later, in 1963, Pettersson himself contracted the same terrible rheumatoid arthritis, which was to afflict him for the rest of his life and which forced him to spend nearly a year in hospital in 1970–1. Yet this experience of suffering never induced in him a trace of self-pity, but instead led to a deep sense of identification with his fellow exiles in life:

I feel I have more affinity with criminals, those who are called criminals, than with other people, not because of what is called their criminality, but because of their longing for freedom, their anguish and suffering, their *feeling of being outside.*[32]

Perhaps [my music] is a protest against predestination, cruelty towards the individual, the individual without a chance.[33]

Lamenting in music in this way could run the risk of creating a merely aesthetic representation of people's suffering, and even of implicitly allowing people to ignore that suffering in favour of the enjoyment of art, weeping more at operas or paintings than at the death of children from AIDS. George Steiner has reminded us that under the Nazi regime,

men and women, apparently sane, could flog and incinerate guiltless victims during their working day and recite Rilke, play Schubert or sing Christmas carols with their loved ones in the evening . . . Indeed . . . it is more than arguable that the genius for speculative abstraction, for aesthetic formalism, for disinterested inquiry immune to the roughage of common needs and pursuits which have marked European intellectual, artistic, scientific eminence, disabled our humanity. Where sensibility and understanding are schooled to respond most intensely to the cry in the poem, to the agony in the painting or to the absolute in the philosophic proposition or scientific axiom, the cry in the street may go unheard.[34]

But Pettersson knew that danger all too well:

A good many people do not concern themselves with music and cannot be educated to make music their concern. Most people get along without music and art. We cannot really expect a man dozing while riding on the subway to go to a concert and listen to music. We go out into the world with missionary zeal and believe that we can redeem humanity with music. Experience has taught me that not a single human being can be made a better person through music. The biggest scoundrels I have ever known were deeply musical. Art is irrational – that cannot be denied. Something bursts inside you, and you begin to sing. That's what black people did under slavery and what soldiers do in times of war. It carries them along and gives them the courage to keep going. When we overcome our personal horrors and make art of them, then our music has a message.[35]

It may be worth concluding with some brief reflections on how we may make the prayer of lament our own in any experiences of exile that we ourselves undergo, or as a way of upholding others in theirs. We have already seen that the biblical laments can become powerful resources for imaginative intercession, and many of them, as 'open texts' susceptible to a wide range of applications, can come alive when allowed to inform our response to particular situations. Thus Psalm 55, the prayer of a victim of urban violence, has been persuasively read as reflecting the terrible experience of rape.[36] Psalms 42 and 43, strictly speaking one unit, make a profoundly moving prayer of a priest or minister who recalls past memories of happier times and now finds his or her own faith painfully tested:

My tears have been my bread day and night,
while all day long they say to me, "Where is now your God?"
Now when I think on these things, I pour out my soul:
how I went with the multitude and led the procession to the
   house of God,
With the voice of praise and thanksgiving,
among those who kept holy day.
Why are you so full of heaviness, O my soul . . . ? (Ps. 42:3–6)

The contemporary Danish-Jewish composer Herman Koppel
(1908–98) has used part of Psalm 38 as a vivid articulation of the
lament of Eve on her expulsion from Eden. Psalm 10 is an extraordinarily effective prayer of political protest on the part of any
excluded or oppressed community: the reference to the Lord
reigning in the closing verses is, as in Psalm 13, no easy piety
tacked on to the end but a defiant refusal to submit to the unjust
regime currently in power. Psalm 71 is the prayer of the elderly
person fearful of the future, Psalm 59 could be the prayer of a
victim of racism, Psalm 88 of someone suffering from AIDS. A
prayer like Psalm 56 can be used to articulate one's own experience
of stress, in this case understanding the enemies about whom the
psalmist speaks as those internal pressures that both depress and
oppress the person praying. And the short sixty-first Psalm expresses with simplicity and directness the experience of exile, with
the beautiful image of God as a fellow traveller, a flying bird under
whose wings we may find temporary refuge on our journey:

Hear my crying, O God,
and listen to my prayer.
From the end of the earth I call to you with fainting heart;
O set me on the rock that is higher than I . . .
Let me dwell in your tent for ever
and take refuge under the cover of your wings. (Ps. 61:1–2, 4)

Some of the biblical laments may even offer us a window into
the suffering of a loving Creator. Thus, one section of the twelfth
chapter of the Book of Jeremiah appears to be a lament on the part
of God:

I have forsaken my house,
   I have abandoned my heritage;

58

I have given the beloved of my heart
into the hands of her enemies . . . (Jer. 12:7)

And texts from Lamentations are familiar to Christians as part of the *Improperia* or Reproaches that are traditionally used in the western Church during the liturgy of Good Friday. Christians have for generations associated Psalm 142 with the prayer of Christ in the tomb, and the bleakest of all the prayers of lament, Psalm 88, gives us an opportunity to enter deeply into the mystery of Christ's passion during Holy Week (as do the Psalms of the *Hallel*, or Passover Psalms, numbers 113–18, which will have been sung by Christ and his disciples before entering Gethsemane).

The biblical laments are not, of course, all lengthy or poetic: some of the most powerful and allusive of them are among the briefest. The prayer of St Peter ('Lord, save me!') as he begins to sink after stepping out of the boat and failing to keep his eyes on Jesus has for centuries sustained countless numbers of Christians who like him have found themselves away from home and no longer in control of what is happening to them.[37] Peter's prayer of envy and puzzlement ('Lord, what about him?'[38]) at the moment when Jesus tells him he will be taken where he does not wish to go anticipates the experience of all those in any kind of exile who cannot help but wonder why others are so much more fortunate than they are: why is N. doing so well when I'm not? And the prayers of the Virgin Mary and other women in Scripture express with striking directness and honesty the experience of the exile: 'how can this be?' 'Child, why have you treated us like this?' 'Where do you get that living water?' 'Lord, do you not care?' 'Lord, if you had been here, my brother would not have died.' The image of St Joseph taking Mary with her child on their lonely journey of exile to Egypt as asylum seekers fleeing from an oppressive ruler remains perhaps *the* defining icon, for Christians, of the spirituality of exile.

Yet the creation of lament in exile need not be restricted to sacred texts. Many contemporary writers and composers have extensively enriched our resources in this regard, from some of the prayers of the French abbé Michel Quoist to more recent work by Janet Morley, John Bell, Brian Wren, and others.[39] Many will seek to write, dance, paint or compose their own laments, drawing on the rich treasury of images and possibilities available in the

59

Judaeo-Christian tradition. And Christians as well as many others will continue to be disturbed as well as enriched, in their own experience of exile, by the work of a huge range of fellow travellers, who all in different ways echo Emile's sad 'This Nearly was Mine' in giving voice to humanity's experience of bitter disappointment and exclusion. In Auschwitz, the young Hugo Gryn tried to observe Yom Kippur (the Jewish Day of Atonement), reciting the *Kol Nidre* and asking for God's forgiveness:

> but eventually I dissolved in crying. I must have sobbed for hours. Never before or since have I cried with such intensity and then I seemed to be granted a curious inner peace. Something of it is still with me. I believe God was also crying. And I understood a bit of the revelation that is implicit in Auschwitz. It is about man and his idols. God, the God of Abraham, could not abandon me, only I could abandon God.[40]

In 1973 the Iraqi woman poet Nazik al'Mala'ika wrote 'The Hijrah [Migration]' to God which includes these haunting lines:

> I found you standing in the essence of a song,
> and in the sadness of the gloom of autumn.
> I found you in the wound of a thirsty flower,
> I found you in the nighttime recitations of the Quran.
> And you built a nest under the veil of darkness
> for a frightened lark and a homeless turtledove,
> their bones folded in sadness,
> for a refugee woman whose bones are folded on sadness,
> for an emigrating caravan, expelled from their homes . . .
> And you hang a moon in the sky of our being,
> and you give it to the misty night of sorrows,
> and you give it to a thirsty grove,
> its plantings forgotten by the rain.[41]

The prayer of lament, then, may take many forms, from a complex and extended poem or work of art to the briefest cry for help. All of them have in common an unflinching honesty in the face of the baffling collision between faith and experience; a childlike boldness in directing our consequent questions towards God, however silent God appears to be; and above all a refusal to permit that bafflement to have the last word. And its relevance to the condition of exile can hardly be overstated: again and again, asylum seekers and others have testified to the fact that, even if or when they arrive at a place of refuge, no one wants to listen to them:

"You can only answer questions they ask – e.g. according to what the interviewer wanted to hear, not how you wanted to express it yourself."

"You're called one at a time [in immigration detention centres]. For admission procedures. Photographs (fingerprints have been taken already). They open a file, give a prison number . . . I have suffered so much. This is what I've been waiting for [to talk about what happens] . . ."

"Even when you go to the GP, they don't take you. We want someone to listen to us, it is a relief when you talk what you feel. 'You are asylum seeker,' they are telling us – when they say this word, we suffer a lot. You can understand from their eyes . . . "[42]

"I love this country very much because it gave me a new life. But when I am sick I feel the loneliness of an exile. In my country when you are sick, relatives and friends come and stay all day. They cook, they clean house, they feed you. Here everybody is so busy they hardly have time to say hello to one another."[43]

In the principal art gallery in Birmingham there is a painting by the Pre-Raphaelite artist Ford Madox-Brown (1821–93). Entitled 'The Last of England', it shows a couple sitting on the crowded deck of a ship (called, appropriately enough, the *Eldorado*), their faces suffused with sadness as they look back at the white cliffs of Dover, the last sight of the country from which they are emigrating. The woman's left hand, just visible through the folds of her grey coat, is cradling the tiny hand of a baby hidden beneath the coat. There are no words, yet this painting is a lament as eloquent as any that have been written. And it is only in our determined refusal to turn away from such sadness, only in our insistence on giving voice in our prayers to the continuing pain of our world, that we can even begin to help all who journey from home into exile to do so with hope and not with fear.

## CHAPTER FIVE

# *The Big Rock Candy Mountain*
## *Keeping the Sabbath in Exile*

In the late 1920s an American called Harry McLintock recorded a song which he may also have composed. It remained relatively obscure until it was re-recorded, in a slightly altered form, by the great Burl Ives (1909–95) twenty years later (and no one who has ever heard it could forget Ives' rendering of the line 'The buzzin' of the bees'). This is how that later version went:

> On a summer's day
> In the month of May,
> A burly bum came a-hiking:
> Down a shady lane
> Near the sugar-cane,
> He was looking for his liking.
> As he strode along,
> He sang a song
> of the land of milk and honey,
> Where a bum can stay
> for many a day,
> And he wouldn't need any money.
> > Oh, the buzzin' of the bees
> > And the cigarette trees,
> > The soda-water fountain,
> > Where the lemonade springs,
> > And the bluebird sings,
> > On the Big Rock Candy Mountain.

> On the Big Rock Candy Mountain,

62

The cops have wooden legs,
The bulldogs all have rubber teeth,
The hens lay soft boiled eggs.
The farmers' trees are full of fruit,
The barns are full of hay.
Oh, I want to go
Where there ain't no snow,
Where the sleet don't fall,
Where the wind don't blow,
In that Big Rock Candy Mountain.
Oh, the buzzin' of the bees . . .

It is clear from the original version of the song, which added a 'lake of gin' to the politically incorrect 'cigarette trees', that it was all about a hobo's idea of paradise.[1] The hobo, or 'burly bum' in the song, was originally an itinerant worker, a member of a particular sub-culture of homeless American migrants who followed the railways westwards seeking work: their numbers increased enormously during the Great Depression of the late 1920s and 1930s. They may not appear to be much different from the 'two drifters off to see the world' whom we encountered in 'Moon River'. But the sunny cheerfulness of 'The Big Rock Candy Mountain' should not deceive us: few embraced the hobo's life for fun, or out of choice, let alone in order to see the world. It is no part of the argument of this book to trivialize exile: it is, for the most part, a painful, desperate place or condition to be in – so much so that sometimes death is preferable, as Job pointed out.[2] Singing is one of the few spiritual resources available to the exile, and (as we have seen) in some situations even that is impossible: how shall we sing the Lord's song in a strange land?

And yet, again and again, especially (though not exclusively) in the history of the people of God, we encounter a striking paradox: that it was precisely *in exile* that the boldest, most creative, most defiant dreams of a new and different future were born. Unlike 'California Dreamin'', 'The Big Rock Candy Mountain' is not nostalgic: the hobo has no idealized past to look back on. But he can still dream of another world, where the police would leave him alone and the bitter cold of the American winter would be replaced by his own version of the biblical land of milk and honey: fertile fields and

63

sunshine and plenty of all he most wanted. And he can give voice to his passionate longing to get there. Plenty of others before and since have done the same, from little Ivo Katz whose poem from Terezín concentration camp we noted earlier, to Martin Luther King telling his followers in Memphis, on the eve of his assassination, that he had been to the mountain top and seen the promised land. The Bible knows many such visions infused with longing, many with the rural imagery of 'The Big Rock Candy Mountain':

> May the pastures of the wilderness flow with goodness
> and the hills be girded with joy.
> May the meadows be clothed with flocks of sheep
> and the valleys stand so thick with corn
> that they shall laugh and sing. (Ps. 65:12–13)

Before looking at some of them in a little more detail, however, a prior question arises: how can exiles keep going in the meantime, before there can be any possibility of their dreams being realized? After all, the prophet Jeremiah made it clear to the exiles in Babylon that they were there for the long haul.[3] Somehow they had to learn the difficult art, which in one form or another all exiles must acquire, of adaptation without conformity: they were to seek the welfare of the people among whom they were living, yet remain culturally and spiritually distinctive. This adaptation is part of the process of evolution, whereby creatures or organisms adjust over time to new conditions. But they may have millennia in which to do this, whereas the exile needs to be able to adapt more swiftly if he or she is to survive at all. The psychiatrist Viktor Frankl, who endured three years in Nazi concentration camps, wrote of the overriding need for people in such situations to construct some form of meaning or pattern, which can not only help the person survive the present, but also point towards some kind of better future, and which must therefore not just be something 'emerging from existence itself but rather something confronting existence'.[4]

This is extraordinarily hard. One Sudanese woman arriving as an asylum seeker in the United Kingdom wrote:

"Generally in life, you have goals, something to cling onto. If you are asylum seeker, you have nothing, you feel emptiness –

64

you don't know where you will be. You fear for your life. Coming from such a background with community, sense of belonging, with the support of an extended family and neighbours, then you come here alone, alienated, it's really indescribable . . ."[5]

And a Vietnamese woman, in exile in the United States, wrote:

"I now realize that people cannot change as quickly as their setting. They transform themselves outwardly, but their essence does not change. The women who come here from Vietnam cannot adapt to the conditions here . . . We can pick up American habits, eat fruit for lunch, drink coffee: we can even call ourselves American, but we are still products of our own culture . . . We have to know who we are and not change our basic nature because of the requirements of the new environment."[6]

It is crucial for those in exile to be helped to create a sense of home, however transient, where they are, for otherwise the sheer sense of dislocation can be so overwhelming as to induce despair.[7] 'Exile,' wrote a Palestinian woman, 'is a no-man's land, where one belongs fully nowhere.'[8] In exile, you somehow have to create what a Malawian woman calls 'the dual consciousness of an exile', the ability to inhabit two different worlds simultaneously – where you are now, and where you have come from, or long to be.[9] It need be neither expensive nor difficult to make places of exile – detention centres, hospital bed spaces and waiting rooms, prison cells, temporary accommodation – more welcoming, more reflective of the uniqueness of those using them, than they normally are. It is not easy for those who work in such places to realize how disabling the anonymity, the bureaucracy, the sheer *noisiness* of so many of them can be for those who have no choice but to enter them, and who will often spend hours or even months waiting in them.

One enduring example of a resource to help people to adapt without conforming to the condition of exile is the sabbath. The origins of this ancient Jewish practice of keeping holy time are by no means clear; it appears in the opening chapter of Genesis as part of the divine rhythm of creation. Indeed, it is precisely the crowning glory of that creation, the culminating seventh day on which God's work is finished, yet the one day on which God did nothing (Gen. 2:2), underlining the crucial truth that we exist for more than work, and that our work only finds its fulfilment and completion when we stop doing it. It is with good reason that the official *Catechism of the Catholic Church*, citing two biblical texts, describes the sabbath as 'a day of protest against the servitude of work and the worship of money'.[10]

We are so accustomed to the notion of sabbath, or of some comparable holy time, that we easily forget just what a surprising thing it is. And on the seventh day God created . . . absolutely nothing. God didn't even get out of bed. Yet that day was so much more important than all the others that it alone, in the opening chapter of Genesis, is described as being both 'blessed' and 'hallowed' (or 'consecrated', Gen. 2:3) – not even human beings merit that double sanctification. And there is a sense in which the sabbath only retains this subversive dimension when it is celebrated in exile, for only when those observing it are not at home and not in control of what happens to them does the keeping of sabbath time become an act of defiance against the dominant culture. Once it, or its Christian or Islamic or some other equivalent, becomes an established part of the dominant culture, it may gain in universality of observance, but something of that intrinsic defiance is lost. It is, therefore, small wonder that the period of the Babylonian exile was critical to the development of the sabbath, even though the institution itself probably predates it.[11] It is, after all, common for those who are far from home to heighten their sense of identity over against the local dominant culture precisely by keeping observances that help to define them, as (say) Scots in Auckland or Buenos Aires will keep Burns' Night with even more vigour than their compatriots at home.

For the Jewish people, then, driven from their ancestral homes and places of worship, the holy *place* was replaced by holy *time*. Indeed, the prophets Jeremiah and Ezekiel both declared that it was in part through a failure to observe the sabbath that the people of God were driven into exile in the first place, and Isaiah vigorously exhorts those who return from exile to ensure that they do observe it.[12] The observance of holy time today, in a fast-moving twenty-four-hour multicultural society, is again an act of protest against unfettered consumerism and endless busyness. But

66

it acquires a far deeper resonance when it is practised in places and conditions of exile: in gulags or concentration camps, in immigration shelters or prisons or hospitals, or in situations of unremitting despair. It is hard for those who are 'time-poor' to understand the sheer grey hopelessness of the person in any of these situations of exile, where time hangs heavy and indeterminate, lacking any sense of momentum or purpose. In such a situation, the ability to mark and divide up the time, and so to bring some kind of order out of chaos, can be crucial for survival.

When people keep sabbath time, or some other form of holy time, in this way, they make their own the profound insight of the opening chapter of Genesis: that human beings are not to be defined by their work, still less to be reduced to statistics or stereotypes. Small wonder that the sabbath has sometimes been described as 'a palace in time': every seventh day, writes one Jewish scholar, 'the Israelite renounces his autonomy and affirms God's dominion over him.'[13] Even if it has to be kept in secret, and marked out only in tiny and unobtrusive ways, its observance represents an act of defiant hope over against the dominant culture, an example of the Beirut hostage Brian Keenan's observation: 'I am still and always will be amazed at the qualities men find in themselves when they have only themselves in which to find a source of life.'[14] And this sense of an interior dynamic existing deep within the self is expressed by one Jewish scholar, who says that for early Jewish rabbis the sabbath was 'a secret place, so to speak, where strict regulation of behaviour and the rigorous enforcement of taboo were combined with a kind of serenity and gratification of body and spirit that would have been the envy of the world if only the world had discovered it.'[15]

The core meaning of the sabbath is to be found in the Pentateuch. At its heart is simply the notion of rest and cessation from work: in the Book of Exodus, we are told that 'on the seventh day [the Lord] rested, and was refreshed' (31:17) – the word 'sabbath' derives from the Hebrew verb 'to rest', whilst the root meaning of the word translated 'was refreshed' is 'caught his breath'. Of the fourteen references to the sabbath in Exodus, all of them are about the cessation of work: none relate to worship, although the Ten Commandments do stipulate that the sabbath day is to be kept holy (Exod. 20:8).

67

But the sabbath is not only about rest. It is also about *memory*, which connects us here with the significance of memory and stories in exile explored earlier. Exodus tells us that the sabbath is itself to be 'remembered' ('Remember the sabbath day, and keep it holy', 20:8), and that we are to keep it in memory of God's seventh-day rest (20:11). The version of the Ten Commandments to be found in the Book of Deuteronomy again connects the sabbath with the shared memory of the people of God; but there the specific event to be remembered on the sabbath is not the creation of the universe, but the liberating event of the Exodus: 'Remember that you were a slave in the land of Egypt, and the Lord your God brought you out from there with a mighty hand and an outstretched arm; therefore the Lord your God commanded you to keep the sabbath day' (5:15).

Part of the keeping of the sabbath, then, is to participate in the divine rest that marks the climax of the process of creation, and thus to make that continuing creative process your own: to appropriate its dynamic for your own life.[16] And part of it is to call consciously to mind the saving work of God in drawing us out of slavery and exile: here, too, the active remembering of past events, both in your own life and in the story of the people of God, makes possible an equally active anticipation of what God still longs to do. To keep sabbath is to remember that exile, whatever form it takes, *is not right*, and that God is a God of homecoming, a God who set people free from slavery in a foreign land and is constantly seeking to do the same today. Keeping the sabbath, then, means ensuring that on one day of the week (for Christians, usually Sunday) you will do no work: you will rest and play, but you will also reflect: where is the Creator Spirit at work in my life, seeking to draw new meaning and hope out of unformed chaos? And what are the occasions in my life where I experienced the power of the Exodus, a profound sense of being set free from something that held me in thrall? From what might God want to set me free today?

It is in the Book of Leviticus that the most interesting material relating to the sabbath and exile is to be found. This rarely read book, the heart of the priestly *torah*, is best understood as a very particular kind of 'portable sanctuary' – in effect, as the social anthropologist Mary Douglas has argued, as a 'temple in written

68

form', providing the Jews in exile with not only a set of moral, spiritual and liturgical guidelines within which to define themselves over against the dominant culture of Babylon, but also an anticipation, a blueprint, of the kind of society they will want to establish once they leave exile.[17] In Leviticus, as in Exodus, the sabbath denotes rest from work, never worship.[18] And, as in the Ten Commandments, the writers of Leviticus integrate the observance of the sabbath within a comprehensive programme of moral and spiritual principles which together articulate their vision of what constitutes holiness: thus, in the nineteenth chapter, the keeping of the sabbath (the only injunction to appear twice) comes, in the first place, between the command to reverence your mother and father and the condemnation of false idols (19:3–4) and, in the second place, between injunctions against prostitution and witchcraft respectively (19:29–31). Keeping holy time, then, becomes one of the defining features of the exile's identity, as well as one of a number of moral ingredients in his or her blueprint for a different life in the future.[19]

And this sense in which keeping sabbath time helps the exile not only to handle the pain of the present but also to begin to imagine, and even to construct, a new future is found in the Levitical stress on the sabbath as being about *restoration*, not just rest. We have already noted that for Jesus restoration was always oriented to the future, not to the past.[20] It is the Book of Leviticus that contains the legislation about the seventh, or sabbatical, year, and about the jubilee year, the fiftieth year that follows seven times seven years. Central to the notion of jubilee is the principle of restoration, both of the land itself, which is to be given its own 'solemn rest' (25:5), and of people who had become indebted to others, and who in the jubilee year are to be allowed the opportunity to buy back their lost status (25:40). As with the legislation concerning the sabbath, it is not only human beings who are to be given this opportunity of rest and restoration, but our fellow creatures, and the land as well.[21] We have seen already that in the Jewish tradition there could be no return to an imagined ideal past: to return to your ancestral home, or to be restored to your lost status, could never simply be a recovery of the *status quo ante*, just as the prophets promised that the new temple to be built after the exile would exceed the old one.[22]

The sabbath, then, points us towards a new future: it is, as a later Jewish text will put it, 'a mirror of the world to come'.[23] In the New Testament, the writer of the Letter to the Hebrews, echoing the relationship between the sabbath rest and the creation of the universe found in Exodus, declares that 'a sabbath rest still remains for the people of God; for those who enter God's rest also cease from their labours as God did from his. Let us therefore make every effort to enter that rest, so that no one may fall through such disobedience as theirs' (4:9–11). And this notion of the sabbath as anticipating the world to come is found frequently in patristic writers. Towards the end of his *City of God*, Augustine says that living in the heavenly city 'will truly be the greatest sabbath, a sabbath that has no evening' and compares it to the divine rest on the seventh day in Genesis 1–2. And he continues,

> We ourselves shall be the seventh day, when we shall be filled and refreshed by [God's] blessing and sanctification . . . Restored by him and perfected by greater grace we shall rest for ever, and see always that he is God, and we shall be filled with him when he himself shall be all in all.[24]

In his commentary on the Song of Songs, Bede tells his fellow Christians that they of all people should grieve least during the labours of our earthly exile, since they are hastening through it towards the vision of eternal peace.[25]

The keeping of the sabbath, then, is something enjoined on individuals, families and communities, and through them to the land and to other creatures, so that the balance, rhythm and wholeness for which everything was created might be restored. For Christians, Jesus' promise to give rest to all who come to him, for his yoke is easy and his burden light, is an invitation to discover the fullness of sabbath rest and restoration in a relationship with him; his ministry of healing on the sabbath was intended precisely to fulfil the vision of the sabbath found in the *torah* by restoring a new future to those who would otherwise have had nothing to which to look forward.[26]

And yet the sabbath is not enough. By definition, it presupposes a context in which most of the rest of the time is devoted to work. Many exiles are suddenly pitched into a situation where they are denied the opportunity to do the one thing they most want to do: to work. Two young Iranian asylum seekers in Birmingham, granted temporary leave to remain in the UK but unable to work, decided none the less to show their gratitude to the host country for allowing them to stay by making a sponsored cycle ride from Glasgow to Birmingham in order to raise money for the local children's hospital. But a young black South African doctor, also granted temporary leave to remain in the UK but waiting well over a year for permission to work, and with a sick child to maintain, wrote to me:

I do not receive any benefits, including Child Benefits; because I do not have a National Insurance number (NI). To get a NI number I have to have a job offer and Home Office documents which clearly state that I can work in the country. For the same reason I cannot apply for [my child's] pre-school grant, which she qualifies for because she does go to nursery and she has started her pre-school year. I am also unable to register for the M.Sc. in Infectious Diseases without a salary . . . I am not in a hurry to return to South Africa. If I could work, I would be able to support myself and pay for my studies. I would even be in a better position to help my nephews and nieces with their college fees. Of course the experience and qualifications will guarantee me a good job upon my return to South Africa. [But] I am now finding it difficult to justify my continuing in this country. I am being denied the right to live a decent life (not allowed to work). I am becoming destitute: I cannot pursue my studies . . . I have been thinking of returning to South Africa . . .[27]

So often we fail, both as a Church and as a society, to honour the gifts and contributions of the stranger and the exile. And we are infinitely the poorer for it, for so often it is the strangers and the exiles themselves who discover from within themselves an astonishing capacity to imagine a new and better future, not only for themselves but for others too, even when there is no sign whatever of it coming into being.

We may conclude by reflecting on this phenomenon. It is first worth asking the question: why is it so important for those in conditions of exile to be able to look forward? In part, this is because it is precisely fear of the future that has led them into exile in the first place. For economic migrants and asylum seekers, the future held no hope at all: indeed, it is only by a concerted attempt on the part of the world's wealthier countries to create economic and political conditions which will encourage people to remain at home that the problem of mass migration will ever be resolved. Fear dominates the lives of those who are driven into exile: fear for themselves, for their children, and for all they hold dear. Furthermore, for many in exile it is impossible not to live to some degree in the past, either reliving nightmares or recalling halcyon days now irretrievably lost. One unmarried mother trapped in a deprived Glasgow housing estate said: 'Justin [her new husband] was great. I have lived a lot of my life in the past. I am still insecure. Social work has made me live in the past by always looking at how I used to treat Miranda. Justin has made me live in the present.'[28]

The ability, then, to begin to envisage a different future is a way of defying the seeming impossibility of any kind of change ever happening – and of defying that impossibility precisely when it seems most set in stone. We have already looked at an example of this in the closing chapters of the Book of Isaiah.[29] There is space to consider one more, in the book which concludes the New Testament. We know little about John, the author of the Book of Revelation, other than that he appears to have been in exile on the island of Patmos because of his faith in Jesus.[30] And it was 'on the Lord's day' that he heard a voice telling him to 'Write in a book what you see and send it to the seven churches' (Rev. 1:10–11). John is far from home, not in control of what is happening to him. But he does not write about himself: he seeks to find some meaning in the chaotic violence and the triumph of evil that he sees all around him, and to offer a vision and message of hope to his fellow Christians before it is too late. He exemplifies the Christian concern to subvert exile from within: just when you might expect him to think about himself, he thinks about others – and not only other Christians or even other human beings, but the fate of the entire cosmos. Just when you might expect him to focus nostalgically on the past, he concentrates almost entirely on the future. Just when you might expect him to be overwhelmed by despair, he sets down in writing his vision of a transcendental, universal hope. And if his language and imagery are sometimes shocking and violent, we must remember, as with the great prayers of lament, that John is writing at a time of crisis, a moment of critical urgency, when (as he saw it) nothing less than the fate of the cosmos was hanging in the balance.

For these reasons the Book of Revelation will always disturb comfortable consciences, just as John's opening letters to the seven churches of Asia must have disturbed them. It is about what theologians call 'eschatology' (the study of the future, and of the final end of creation), and no one has defined that better than Eugene Peterson in his study of the Book of Jonah:

> Eschatology is the tool we use to loosen the soil and weed the field . . . [When] Jonah entered Nineveh, . . . he didn't make appreciative comments on the landscape; he let loose with something arrestingly eschatological: 'Yet forty days, and Nineveh shall be overthrown' . . . He didn't accuse them of being evil. He didn't denounce their sin and wickedness. He called into question their future. He introduced eschatology into their now-oriented religion, their security-obsessed present.[31]

Like the message of Jonah, John of Patmos is uncompromising in what he tells his fellow Christians. They are to 'hang on in there': they are to wait, to remain faithful to what they have been taught, to repent of where they have failed and to change their lives and their churches before it is too late. They cannot go on as they are. But (and this is crucial) their waiting is not to be the apathetic, dispirited waiting of those who have no hope, but the active, alert, expectant waiting of those who know that evil will not have the last word. 'The time is near,' says John (1:3).

And his primary direction to his fellow Christians is not to *repent*, important though that is – to discard their 'now-oriented religion, their security-obsessed present' – but to *praise*. Praising God's coming reign in places of exile collapses time, lifting God's new future into the present, and defying the iron certainties of the status quo just when they appeared to be omnipotent. This is how John expresses it:

> After this I heard what seemed to be the loud voice of a great multitude in heaven, saying, 'Hallelujah! Salvation and glory and power to our God, for his judgements are true and just; he has judged the great whore who corrupted the earth with her

fornication, and he has avenged on her the blood of his servants.' Once more they said, 'Hallelujah! The smoke goes up from her for ever and ever.' And the twenty-four elders and the four living creatures fell down and worshipped God who is seated on the throne, saying, 'Amen. Hallelujah!' (19:1–4)

This is the language of apocalyptic: otherworldly, centred upon heaven more than earth, anticipating a new cosmos and a new future which those who have remained faithful will share. Yet the otherworldliness is deceptive: salvation and glory and power belong to 'our God', not to the Roman emperor. And John makes this grand declaration of God's victory even before the final decisive battle with the forces of evil has taken place. Christians are to fall down and worship God and celebrate that victory even while there is no sign that it will ever happen.

And, once it has happened, John concludes his book with a vision of the heavenly city, a transformation of both heaven and earth since this new city 'comes down out of heaven from God' even though it is a renewed version of the earthly city of Jerusalem (21:2). In this city God will 'dwell', or 'pitch his tent' (21:3): the nomad God and a nomadic people will be nomads no longer: everyone will *belong*. This city is not the same as the garden with which the Bible opens, though it does contain the tree of life found once in Eden (22:2).[32] It will be a *restored* city, rooted in the past history of the people of God (with the names of the twelve tribes of Israel inscribed on its gates, 21:12), yet welcoming all the world's peoples and belonging to them too. It will be a *holy* city, yet its holiness will consist not in the separation of sacred from secular but of the good from the evil: only those who 'practise abomination or falsehood' will be excluded (21:27). And in this city, everyone will be priestly and royal; there will be no need of a temple or narrowly religious building – religion and culture will become one.[33] It will be a *beautiful* city, shining with jewels and with streets 'transparent as glass' (21:21) – a place people will long to come to and inhabit. It will be an *inclusive* city, a place created 'for the healing of the nations' (22:2), a place to which people will bring all the glory and honour of the world's diversity of nations (21:26), and in which only evil will be excluded: there will be gates, but they will never close (21:25).

Where does this amazing, compellingly attractive vision of the future of the universe come from? Not from an ecclesiastical committee, nor from the leisured reflections of the prosperous or the powerful, but from an individual in exile. This is not to suggest that the vision sprang entirely from the experience of one person: John of Patmos will have drawn on the shared memories and stories of his fellow Jews – the great prophecies of Isaiah, and the universal vision of Psalm 87 – and set his own experience of exile in that context.[34] And, like the Jews by the waters of Babylon, John demonstrates the extraordinary capacity of those in exile to subvert the iron bars of their condition and invite others to join them in dreaming of how things could be. The powerful, and the religious, will not always esteem such visions, since radical change will be demanded of them if the visions are to be achieved. Yet without such visions to animate and direct them, the world's religions will become dull or even dangerous, more interested in perpetuating their own institutions than in making the city of God a reality on earth.

Christianity has a unique contribution to make here, and not only because both its sacred texts and its history offer such rich resources for understanding the mystery of exile and migration in a world as rootless as our own. For at the epicentre of Christian faith is the conviction that God embraced exile in order to rescue us from ours, that God became homeless in order to bring all of us home, and that in the life and death and resurrection of Jesus we are not only offered a paradigm for finding hope and meaning in our own journeys of exile, but also set free to embrace and make our own the vision of a new cosmos which he came to proclaim. But embracing that vision will be immensely costly, since it will demand, first, a recognition that we cannot go on as we are, comfortably preoccupied with our own institutional survival – and, second, a willingness to reverence and seek out the least likely people in our midst – the exiles and the nomads of our own day – and discover precisely from them the truth of how we may make Christ's vision a reality.

There are signs of hope, even in the midst of a world that is currently as violent and chaotic as the world John looked out on from his exile's window on Patmos. During Refugee Week recently, in Birmingham as in other cities across the country and the world, members of different migrant communities joined to celebrate the right of sanctuary and the vision of a society united in diversity: Afghans, Bosnians, Sudanese, Rwandans and countless others danced and sang and shared their stories and their hopes. In the cathedral, a Jewish music group sang of their people's long journeys of exile while Iranians, Iraqi Kurds and many others applauded before singing of theirs too. The hobo dreaming of the Big Rock Candy Mountain was not interested in changing the world: only of escaping from the grim exile in which he found himself. But – and this is God's great surprise – it is the exile's vision that can renew the cosmos, for only those who have, in some sense or other, stepped out in faith without knowing where they were going are free enough from our obsession with security and control to dream of a different world.

# NOTES

## Chapter One: What Is Exile?

1 *Beginning Now* (London: Collins, 1971), p. 40.
2 'El olvidado asombro de estar vivos', from 'Piedra de Sol' (1957), in Octavio Paz, *Configurations* (London: Jonathan Cape, 1971), pp. 22–3.
3 Interview in the magazine *Inexile* 22 (2002), (published by the UK Refugee Council), p. 8.
4 Interview in the magazine *Inexile* 27 (2003) (published by the UK Refugee Council), p. 23.
5 D.H. Lawrence, *Sons and Lovers* (Harmondsworth: Penguin, 1948), pp. 12–13.

## Chapter Two: Moon River

1 Hala Deeb Jabbour, quoted by Mahnaz Afkhami in *Women in Exile* (Charlottesville: Virginia University Press, 1994), p. 63.
2 The friendship of Ruth and Naomi reflects the comment of a Chilean woman in exile who wrote that 'in all this I have learned that women are deeper, stronger than men in their relationships. They are capable of intimacy without too much preparation, too much hedging and insurance. During the period of exile, the women who had never worked, never supported a family, women with little education picked up the pieces of their lives and started building. They were the pillars of the family structure. They held everything together' (Marjorie Agosin, quoted by Afkhami in *Women in Exile*, p. 149).
3 It is worth noting that the overwhelming majority of the world's refugees and 'displaced persons' are women and children. See Afkhami, *Women in Exile*, p. vii.

4 Stanley Stewart, *In the Empire of Genghis Khan: a Journey among Nomads* (London: HarperCollins, 2000), p. xvii.

5 *ibid.*, pp. 168–9. For a wonderfully vivid description of contemporary Mongolia, see Louisa Waugh, *Hearing Birds Fly* (London: Abacus, 2003).

6 Stewart, *In the Empire of Genghis Khan*, pp. 257–8.

7 The Greek words here translated 'strangers' and 'aliens' are *xenoi* and *paroikoi* respectively: the latter word is used in the Septuagint, or Greek version of the Hebrew Bible, to translate *ger*.

8 There is much debate about the origin of Psalm 119. Hans-Joachim Kraus describes its spirituality as a *theologia viatorum* (*Psalms 60–150: A Continental Commentary*, trans. by Hilton C. Oswald, Minneapolis: Fortress, 1993, p. 420). On the other hand, Alfons Deissler sees the psalm as 'an anthology of wisdom sayings that originated in a (post-exilic) "learned circle" of scholarly scribal wisdom' (*Psalm 119(118) und seine Theologie*, Munich: Karl Zink, 1955) – though Deissler's argument fails to take sufficient account of the psalm's constant references to journeying, and its intensely emotional character. For this writer, the most convincing argument about the psalm appears in Will Soll's monograph *Psalm 119: Matrix, Form and Setting* (Catholic Biblical Quarterly Monograph Series 23, Washington DC: Catholic Biblical Association of America, 1991): Soll suggests that the psalm is either exilic or shortly post-exilic, largely as a result of its close similarity with Lamentations 3, which was clearly written after the destruction of the first Temple and prior to the completion of the second (p. 143). He underlines the weaknesses in Deissler's argument (for example, the surprising absence of any references to the precise content of *torah* in the psalm, which would seem strange if the psalm were an anthology of scribal wisdom but much less so if the psalmist could take that for granted and seek instead to hold onto the reality and companionship of *torah* as a whole in exile) (see pp. 64–5).

9 The comments of Hans Urs von Balthasar are worth recalling here: speaking of Psalm 119, he writes that what the psalmist speaks of is 'no congealed "law", but existence in the pure and utterly vulnerable receiving of each word that goes forth from the mouth of God, even when this mouth remains invisible for him. Such existence means hanging on God's lips, trusting in his commandments, walking in the path of his instructions, and loving the word, the directive and prescription, the decree and the command, the order and the promise unconditionally with the same love one has for God himself: and seeing, in this pure grace, sheer goodness. "How sweet are your words to my tongue" (Ps. 119:103)' (*The Glory of the Lord*, vol. 6, trans. by Merikakis and McNeil, Edinburgh: T. & T. Clark, 1991, pp. 382–3).

10 For Lourdes see Ruth Harris, *Lourdes: Body and Spirit in a Secular Age* (Harmondsworth: Penguin, 1999), a study at once academic and personal, and all the more moving for its author's agnosticism.

11 John Hull, *In the Beginning there was Darkness: A Blind Person's Conversations with the Bible* (London: SCM, 2001), p. 49.

12 Spurgeon, *Sermons* (Albany: Ages Software, 1997), 1754:861–2.

13 St John describes the non-Christian Jewish leaders of his own day as either 'the Pharisees' (John 9:13, 15–16, 40) or 'the Jews' (John 9:18–22). We will best convey what he meant, and in the process avoid any hint of antisemitism, and of prejudice against the Pharisees (who were for the most part outstandingly good and devout people), by describing them as the 'religious authorities'.

14 Quoted in *Asylum Voices: Experiences of People Seeking Asylum in the United Kingdom*, ed. Andrew Bradstock and Arlington Trotman (London: Churches Together in Britain and Ireland, 2003), p. 56.

15 'He was seeing, and he wasn't seeing; he was seeing with his eyes, but not yet seeing with his heart' (St Augustine, Sermon 135, trans. by Edmund Hill OP in *The Works of Saint Augustine*, vol. III/4: Sermons 94a–147a, New York: New City, 1992, p. 349).

16 See, for example, Augustine, *Sermons on the Gospel of Saint John*, 44:2, although Augustine suggests that the real baptism takes place when the man 'washes the face of his heart' in his encounter with Jesus, who is 'sent': 'so [Jesus] himself was Siloam. The man blind in heart approached, heard, believed, worshipped, washed his face, saw' (Augustine, Sermon 136:2, ed.cit. in note 15 above, p. 354; Sermon 136C:3, ed.cit. in note 15 above, p. 368; and *Sermons on the Gospel of Saint John* 44:15).

## Chapter Three: California Dreamin'

1 Quoted in Martin Gilbert, *The Holocaust: the Jewish Tragedy* (London: Collins, 1987), p. 262.

2 Alicia Partnoy, quoted in Mahnaz Afkhami, *Women in Exile* (Charlottesville: Virginia University Press, 1994), p. 108.

3 Kenneth Grahame, *The Wind in the Willows* (1908), from chap. 5 ('Dulce Domum').

4 Matthieu Ricard, *The Mystery of Animal Migration* (1968), trans. by Peter J. Whitehead (London: Constable, 1969), p. 194.

5 See Luke 15:11–end.

6 Genesis 3:24.

7 Mark 6:5.

8 Mark 6:3.

9 Jeremiah 29:1–14.

10 Jeremiah 31:23–40. For the whole of this subject, see Walter Brueggemann, *The Land* (Philadelphia: Fortress, 1977), esp. chaps. 6–8.

11 See Ezekiel 47:21–3 and Isaiah 66:18–21.

12 Philip Gourevitch, *We Wish to Inform You That Tomorrow We Will be Killed with Our Families* (London: Picador, 1999), p. 230.

13 Jeremiah 24. See Brueggemann, *The Land*, p. 124.

14 Psalm 89:39, 41, 47.

15 Afkhami, *Women in Exile*, p. 6.

16 'It takes courage to explore the memory, especially in a situation of amnesia like ours . . . The particulars are such an embarrassment to the regime. People who believe the universal myths are easier to administer, for then we are all alike and indeed we are really replaceable parts . . . When we have completely forgotten our past, we will absolutize the present and we will be like contented cows in Bashan who want nothing more than the best of today. People like that can never remember who they are, cannot remember their status as exiles or that home is somewhere else. It takes a powerful articulation of memory to maintain a sense of identity in the midst of exile' (Walter Brueggemann, *Hopeful Imagination*, Philadelphia: Fortress, 1986), p. 102.

17 Brian Keenan, *An Evil Cradling* (London: Hutchinson, 1992), p. 85.

18 Ovid, *Letters from Pontus* 4.ix.41ff, ET by A.L. Wheeler in *Ovid, VI: Tristia; Ex Ponto*, 2nd edn (Loeb Classical Library, Harvard: HUP, 1988), pp. 457–9.

19 Augustine, *Confessions* X.8.14, ET by Henry Chadwick in *Saint Augustine: Confessions* (Oxford: OUP, 1991), pp. 186–7.

20 Augustine, *The Trinity* XIV.4.15, ET by Edmund Hill OP in *Saint Augustine: The Trinity* (Brooklyn, NY: New City (*The Works of Saint Augustine*, I:5), 1991), p. 383.

21 From *I have not seen a butterfly around here: children's drawings and poems from Terezín*, ed. H. Volavkova, ET by Edith Pargeretova (Prague: Jewish Museum, 1993), p. 73.

22 Metropolitan Anthony of Sourozh, 'The Spirituality of Ageing', Occasional Paper no. 4, 3rd edn (Epworth House, Derby: Christian Council on Ageing, 1995), p. 7.

23 Psalm 71:6–7, 9, 18, 20.

# Chapter Four: This Nearly was Mine

1 Edward Said, 'Reflections on Exile' (1984), repr. in *Reflections on Exile and other Literary and Cultural Essays* (London: Granta, 2000), pp. 181–2.

2 Shakespeare, *Macbeth*, Act 4, Scene 3.

3 See Chapter 5.

4 Luke 18:1–8.

5 In *Variations on a Theme: King, Messiah and Servant in the Book of Isaiah* (Carlisle: Paternoster, 1998) Hugh Williamson argues that what we see in Third Isaiah (chaps. 56–66) is a further development of the two earlier sections: where First Isaiah conceived of the (Davidic) king as the key mediator between God and his people, and Second Isaiah of the whole nation of Israel, Third Isaiah conceived of the righteous within Israel (and, fascinatingly, also the righteous among the Gentiles) as being the mediator charged with carrying out God's task. The glorious promises of Second Isaiah have been narrowed to a small segment within Israel, as a way of explaining the otherwise baffling fact that post-exilic Israel did not fulfil the dreams Second Isaiah had for it. Consequently a new stress on individual responsibility begins to develop, and in texts like chap. 56:6–7 and chap. 65 there is little or no distinction between Israelites and Gentiles: what matters is whether or not you are righteous, not whether or not you are Jewish (p. 197). At the very end of the book, in chap. 66:21, even the priests and Levites are described as being drawn from non-Jewish as well as Jewish sources (see p. 199).

6 The theme of God as mother has already appeared in Second Isaiah (42:14).

7 The very last verse of Isaiah is unique in the Hebrew Bible as being a promise of universal annihilation for those who rebel against God (66:24). In some mss. verse 23 is repeated after verse 24 so as not to end the book with an oracle of doom. But in most it is the extraordinary image of the humble worm that has the last word, and with it the stern reminder that people will still be able to choose, for or against God and all that God longs to do in recreating the cosmos.

8 On the idea of those in exile becoming redemptive figures, see N.T. Wright, *The New Testament and the People of God* (London: SPCK, 1992), p. 276.

9 'Exile did not lead Jews in the Old Testament to abandon faith or to settle for abdicating despair, nor to retreat to privatistic religion. On the contrary, exile evoked the most brilliant literature and the most daring theological articulation in the Old Testament' (Walter Brueggemann,

*Cadences of Home: Preaching among Exiles*, Louisville, Ky: Westminster John Knox, 1997, p. 3).

10 Tod Linafelt, *Surviving Lamentations: Catastrophe, Lament and Protest in the Afterlife of a Biblical Book* (Chicago: Chicago University Press, 2000), p. 78.

11 Lamentations 4:10; 5:1–4; 3:43–4.

12 Psalm 69:1–2. Cf. Psalm 42:9, Psalm 88:7–8 and 18–19, and many other similar passages.

13 See Genesis 8 and 17; Deuteronomy 5; Jeremiah 31:31–7; Ezekiel 34:25–31 and 37:15–28; Hebrews 8–9.

14 Psalm 10:1, 4, 11.

15 See esp. Psalm 44:24–end and Psalm 78:65.

16 See esp. Romans 8:14–17; Galatians 4:1–7; Matthew 18:1–14.

17 W. Winnicott, *The Child, the Family, and the Outside World* (Harmondsworth: Penguin, 1964), p. 125.

18 D.W. Winnicott, *Playing and Reality* (London: Tavistock, 1971), p. 71.

19 Anthony Storr, *The School of Genius* (London: André Deutsch, 1988), p. 96.

20 For this, see *ibid.*, chap. 2.

21 This is Winnicott's term: see his *Home is Where We Start From* (Harmondsworth: Penguin, 1986), pp. 39–54.

22 Walter Brueggemann, 'The Costly Loss of Lament', *Journal for the Study of the Old Testament* 36 (1986), p. 64, reprinted in his *The Psalms and the Life of Faith*, ed. Patrick D. Miller (Minneapolis: Fortress, 1995), p. 107.

23 Matthew 23:36–9.

24 Nicholas Wolterstorff, *Lament for a Son*, Preface to 1997 edition (London: SPCK, 1997).

25 See Leviticus 11:17–18.

26 See John Bell, 'The Lost Tradition of Lament' in *Composing Music for Worship*, ed. Stephen Darlington and Alan Kreider (Norwich: Canterbury Press, 2003), pp. 104–16.

27 Quoted by Geary in *Composing Music for Worship*, ed. Darlington and Kreider, p. 135.

28 Compare this with the moving biblical superscription to Psalm 102: 'A prayer of one afflicted, when faint and pleading before the Lord'.

29 Jeremiah 9:17–18. See also 2 Chronicles 35:25, where we are told that 'Jeremiah also uttered a lament for Josiah, and all the singing-men and singing-women have spoken of Josiah in their laments to this day.'

30 Allan Pettersson, from *Barfotasånger och Andra Dikter* (Barefoot Songs), trans. by and quoted in Paul Rapoport, *Opus est: Six Composers from Northern Europe* (London: Kahn & Averill, 1978), p. 111.

31 From an interview with Urban Stenström in 1958 on the first perform-

ance of Pettersson's Third Concerto for String Orchestra, printed as 'Allan Pettersson – komponerande och grubblande son av Söder', in *Nutida Musik* 1:5 (1958), pp. 6–7; trans. by and quoted in *ibid.*, p. 113.

32 From 'Anteckningar', in *Nutida Musik* 4:4 (1960–1), p. 19; trans. by and quoted in *ibid.*, p. 109.

33 Quoted by Göran Bergendal, 'Allan Pettersson? Just det!', in *Röster i Radio* 49 (1968), p. 20, trans. by and quoted in *ibid.*, p. 110.

34 George Steiner, 'Remembering the Future' (address given in King's College Chapel, Cambridge on Remembrance Sunday 1989 and reprinted in *Theology* 93 (1990), p. 439).

35 Allan Pettersson, trans. by Susan Marie Praeder; printed in the CD liner note to accompany the recording of his Symphony No. 13 by the BBC Scottish Symphony Orchestra conducted by Alun Francis, on the CPO label (999 224–2).

36 See Ulrike Bail, ' "O God, hear my prayer": Psalm 55 and Violence against Women', in *Wisdom and Psalms: A Feminist Companion to the Bible (Second Series)*, ed. Athalya Brenner and Carole R. Fontaine (Sheffield Academic Press, 1998), pp. 242–63.

37 Matthew 14:30.

38 John 21:21.

39 Michel Quoist, *Prayers of Life* (Paris, 1954); Brian Wren, *Bring Many Names* (Oxford: OUP, 1989); *Celebrating Women*, ed. Hannah Ward, Jennifer Wild and Janet Morley, new edn (London: SPCK, 1995); Hannah Ward and Jennifer Wild, *Human Rites: Worship Resources for an Age of Change* (London: Mowbray, 1995). The hymns and songs of John Bell are published by Wild Goose Publications, the publishing division of the Iona Community.

40 Hugo Gryn (with Naomi Gryn), *Chasing Shadows* (London: Viking, 2000), p. 251.

41 From *Iraqi Poetry Today*, ed. Daniel Weissbort (Modern Poetry in Translation, 19) (London: King's College, 2003), pp. 126–7.

42 Experiences of overseas asylum seekers arriving in the UK, quoted in *Asylum Voices: Experiences of People Seeking Asylum in the United Kingdom*, ed. Andrew Bradstock and Arlington Trotman (London: Churches Together in Britain and Ireland, 2003), pp. 38 and 46.

43 Samnang Wu, a Cambodian exile, quoted in Mahnaz Afkhami, *Women in Exile* (Charlottesville: Virginia University Press, 1994), p. 187.

# Chapter Five: The Big Rock Candy Mountain

1 Some later versions homogenize the 'cigarette trees' into 'peppermint trees'.

2 See, for example, Job chapter 3.

3 Jeremiah 29.

4 Viktor Frankl, *Man's Search for Meaning*, trans. by Ilse Lasch, revised edn (London: Hodder and Stoughton, 1964), p. 100.

5 Quoted in *Asylum Voices: Experiences of People Seeking Asylum in the United Kingdom*, ed. Andrew Bradstock and Arlington Trotman (London: Churches Together in Britain and Ireland, 2003), p. 58.

6 Ho Ngoc Tran, quoted in Mahnaz Afkhami, *Women in Exile* (Charlottesville: Virginia University Press, 1994), p. 31.

7 Edward Said, writing of exile, has said that 'there is a particular sense of achievement in acting as if one were at home wherever one happens to be' ('Reflections on Exile', in *Reflections on Exile and Other Literary and Cultural Essays*, London: Granta, 2001), p. 186.

8 Hala Deeb Jabbour, quoted in Afkhami, *Women in Exile*, p. 59.

9 Florence Simfukwe, quoted in *ibid.*, p. 123.

10 *Catechism of the Catholic Church* (London: Geoffrey Chapman, 1994), 2172. The Catechism cites Nehemiah 13:15–22, and 2 Chronicles 36:21.

11 For this subject, and for much more wisdom about the sabbath, see the essays by Jewish and Christian scholars in *The Sabbath in Jewish and Christian Traditions*, ed. T.C. Eskenazi, D.J. Harrington sj, and W.H. Shea (New York: Crossroad, 1991).

12 See Jeremiah 17:19–27; Ezekiel 20:11–26 and 22:26; Isaiah 56:2–7 and 58:13–14.

13 Matitiahu Tsevat, *The Meaning of the Book of Job and Other Biblical Studies* (1980), quoted in Walter Brueggemann, *The Psalms and the Life of Faith* (Minneapolis: Fortress, 1995), p. 35.

14 Brian Keenan, *An Evil Cradling* (London: Hutchinson, 1992), p. 266.

15 Robert Goldenberg, 'The Place of the Sabbath in Rabbinic Judaism', in Eskenazi *et al* (eds.), *The Sabbath in Jewish and Christian Traditions*, p. 32.

16 This notion of the sabbath as denoting a recovery of the ancient rhythm of the creation is developed extensively by patristic writers, especially by Augustine (see e.g. *Confessions* 13:35–6; Samuele Bacchiocchi, 'Remembering the Sabbath: the Creation-Sabbath in Jewish and Christian History', in Eskenazi *et al.* (eds.), *The Sabbath in Jewish and Christian Traditions*, p. 79).

17 See Mary Douglas, *Leviticus as Literature* (Oxford: OUP, 1999). In Douglas' view, the writer is also 'teaching the people of Israel to hon-

our in their lives the order of creation, and by doing so to share in its work . . . The smallest case miniaturizes the cosmos, but it is always the same cosmos, constructed on the same principles' (pp. 45–6). In this context, Leviticus extends and elaborates the continuing creative work of God in Genesis 1.

18 In Leviticus 23, the observance of the sabbath is linked with various liturgical festivals, but its primary meaning remains cessation from work.

19 In this connection, see Walter S. Wurzburger, 'A Jewish Theology and Philosophy of the Sabbath', in Eskenazi et al. (eds.), The Sabbath in Jewish and Christian Traditions, p. 146; Walter Brueggemann writes: 'I understand the Sabbath to be a quiet but uncompromising refusal to be defined by the production system of Babylon, so that life is regularly and with discipline enacted as a trusted gift and not as a frantic achievement' (Cadences of Home, Louisville: Westminster John Knox, 1997), p. 8. See also Erhard S. Gerstenberger, Leviticus: A Commentary (Louisville: Westminster John Knox, 1996), p. 266): it was only during the Babylonian exile that the sabbath became a confessional symbol of the first order (cf. Leviticus 23:3): it becomes for the exiled community a symbol of identity (ibid., p. 340).

20 See Chapter 2 above.

21 In the Ten Commandments animals are commanded to rest, as well as the foreigner: 'you, your son or your daughter, your male or female slave, your livestock, or the alien resident in your towns' (Exodus 20:10). Exodus 23:10–13 extends the same privilege to the land during the sabbatical year.

22 See esp. Haggai 2:1–9.

23 Zohar, Genesis 48a; quoted in Eskenazi et al. (eds.), The Sabbath in Jewish and Christian Traditions, p. x.

24 St Augustine, The City of God, Book 22:30, trans. by William M. Green, Loeb Classical Library (Cambridge, Mass.: HUP, 1972), p. 381.

25 In Canticle of Canticles 1:1, p. 195.

26 See Matthew 11:25–30: it is worth noting that Jesus' offer of 'rest' comes immediately before the principal material concerning his attitude to the sabbath in Matthew.

27 Personal letter to the author, published with permission, dated 5 September 2004.

28 Carol, quoted in Bob Holman, Faith in the Poor (Oxford: Lion, 1998), p. 43.

29 See above, Chapter 4.

30 See Revelation 1:9.

31 Eugene Peterson, *Under the Unpredictable Plant* (Chicago: Eerdmans, 1992), pp. 140–2.
32 It is worth noting Christopher Rowland's comment here: 'As we grow ever more fearful about life in our cities, and as people seek escape in some suburban or rural idyll, it is important to be reminded that the fulfilment of God's purposes is centred on a city, a community that reflects God's paradise' (Commentary on Revelation, in *The New Interpreter's Bible*, vol. XII, Nashville: Abingdon, 1998, p. 730).
33 See Revelation 1:6, 5:10 and 21:22.
34 Cf. the remarks of a Chilean woman who wrote that 'being in exile, I have grown from feeling I have no country to accepting the whole world as my country' (quoted by Afkhami in *Women in Exile*, p. 144).